P9-DHR-630

JOY JUICE

Delightful Flavors
Of
JOY in the Lord

By
Joyce J. Ashley

PRESS

Copyright © 2009 by Joyce J. Ashley

Joy Juice
Delightful Flavors of JOY in the Lord
by Joyce J. Ashley

Printed in the United States of America

ISBN 9781615796779

All rights reserved solely by the author. The author guarantees all contents are original and do not infringe upon the legal rights of any other person or work. No part of this book may be reproduced in any form without the permission of the author. The views expressed in this book are not necessarily those of the publisher.

Unless otherwise indicated, Bible quotations are taken from The HOLY BIBLE, NEW INTERNATIONAL VERSION. NIV. Copyright © 1973, 1978, 1984 by International Bible Society. Used by permission of Zondervan. All rights reserved.

Scripture marked AMP is taken from The Amplified Bible. Copyright © 1954, 1958, 1962, 1964, 1965, 1987 by The Lockman Foundation. Used by permission.

Scripture marked ESV is taken from The Holy Bible, English Standard Version. Copyright © 2001 by Crossway Bibles, a division of Good News Publishers. Used by permission.

Scripture marked KJV is taken from The King James Version of the Bible.

Scripture marked NKJV is taken from The New King James Version. Copyright © 1982 by Thomas Nelson, Inc. Used by permission.

Scripture marked NASB is taken from The New American Standard Bible. Copyright © 1960, 1962, 1963, 1968, 1971, 1972, 1973, 1975, 1977, 1995 by The Lockman Foundation. Used by permission.

www.xulonpress.com

Thank You

❦

Special thanks to my awesome editor, Jennifer Hanchey from Franklin, Tennessee. Her guidance and encouragement helped to make the writing of this book a joyful experience.

Praise for
JOY JUICE

✳

"**W**hen Joyce first approached me about starting *Joy Juice* as a radio ministry, I embraced the idea and decided to lend my support. I didn't realize at the time that I would become a listener and fan of the show on my own radio stations, as well. Joyce's unrelenting cheerfulness is catching and is something which comes across in her programs. It has indeed brought joy to me and to many of our listeners. I am pleased that now her readers will have an opportunity to experience *Joy Juice*, too!"

John Higgs, President
Broadcast South Radio Group
Georgia

"There's an old English proverb that says, 'A joy that's shared is a joy made double.' In this delightful book, Joyce Ashley reminds us of the availability of God's joy and its practical outworking in our lives. As you read these encouraging words, may they point you to the Savior who is the true Giver of all joy. Today, choose joy, and double your portion as you share the joy juice of Christ with others."

Terry Tidwell
WAFT Radio
Valdosta, Georgia

"It's no wonder that Joyce would write on the subject of biblical joy. It exudes from her life, and she has put her journey into words so that we can also discover and maintain a life of joy. That's why I highly recommend *Joy Juice*. It's refreshing, enlightening and supported by the Word of God. If you've tried to create joy by your own efforts and have failed, then *Joy Juice* is for you. True joy is a direct result from knowing and serving God. Joyce teaches us how to accomplish both."

Micca Campbell
Proverbs 31 Speaker
Author of
An Untroubled Heart

"Joy is something we all long for and at times even attempt to create, but in the end, it is a gift from God. This blessing is available at all times and during all situations. In *Joy Juice* you will find practical reminders of this truth and will be encouraged to live in the JOY of the Lord."

Jill Beran
Co-Author of
Letters from Leanne—The Beauty of a Spiritual Mother-Daughter Relationship

"Are you parched, dehydrated and under-nourished spiritually? Then this book is the key to filling you up and helping you out. It's a joyful experience of words, buffet style—all you can eat and drink—right in the palm of your hands. Delicious and nutritious! That is what I call a meal of words to feast on. I naturally started to smile and my heavy load lightened as I read one page after another. Joyce has a natural gift of turning the Word of God into something I could feel, see and taste, all in one sitting. I came to the book with a heavy heart and left feeling filled up with the Fruit of the Spirit. What a wonderful gift she has been given! I highly recommend *Joy Juice* to anyone thirsting for more. Whether you are a seasoned believer or a brand new Christian, you will find this cup of juice satisfying to your soul. Sip! Drink! It's fresh and fruity! Who would not want more?"

Cris Nole
Writer/Speaker
Daughters of Destiny
Proverbs 31 "She Speaks" Graduate

"When you hear Joyce speak, it's as if each word is about to burst forth in a melody of joy. You feel that melody as you read her book, too. *Joy Juice* will encourage you and make you want the contagious joyful spirit she has because of Jesus. I cannot imagine anything better than having a bunch of Joyce Ashleys impacting our world. Joyce is a dynamic speaker and writer. Sit down with her book, and get ready to drink the most delicious drink you have ever experienced. No one is more qualified than Joyce to write a book on joy because she lives what she speaks. Drink up and *enjoy **Joy Juice**!*"

B J Funk
Speaker and Writer
Author of
The Dance of Life:
Invitation to a Father-Daughter Dance
&
In This Very Hour

DEDICATION

This book is lovingly dedicated to my parents who were life-long models of joy. My father's name was Pleasant, and my mother's name is Mary. Now, how appropriate is that? With a "pleasant" dad and a "merry" mom, it's no wonder that I have joy in my heart. (And they chose to name me "JOYce". Do you think God may have had a plan?) Truly, God blessed my siblings and me with a Godly home where there was lots of laughter and joy in the Lord. Even through the tough times, our parents remained steadfast in their faith and demonstrated an inexpressible joy.

I also dedicate this book to our three children: Todd, Eric, and Alison; our daughters-in-love: Annette and Kathryn; and our adorable grandchildren: Nathan, Naomi, Will, and all the sweet grandbabies to come. From the depths of my heart, I say to them, "Through your lives, God has shown me a dimension of His love that I would have never known. It is incomprehensible that He loves us more than I love you. I praise Him for the joy He has lavished on me through you."

Finally, but oh, so joyfully, I give thanks to our Lord for gifting me with the love of my life, Patrick Mitchell Ashley. My wonderful husband has been my encouragement, my support, my patient sounding board, and my partner in joy. God knew that I needed his calm, thoughtful demeanor to balance my Type A personality. Pat, these past thirty-seven years of marriage have overflowed with joy. Thanks for laughing with me often, letting me cry when my "cup runneth over," (Psalm 23:5 KJV) and always supporting me in my pursuit of God's plan for my life. I look forward to sharing at least thirty-seven more wonderful years with you, and then a joyful eternity.

Table of Contents

Introduction

"Rejoice in the Lord always. I will
say it again: Rejoice!"
Philippians 4:4

We read this verse and many times wonder: "Is it really possible to rejoice *always*? How can we be joyful when we are in the midst of heartache and trial? Are we less of a Christian when we fall short and find ourselves lacking joy?

You hold in your hands a labor of love—love for my Lord and Savior, Jesus Christ. He has given me a passion to share His love with others because that love is the only way to experience genuine joy. Each word in this book was planted first in my heart by the Giver of Joy. As JoyJoy Ministries has expanded over the past couple of years, it was evident that His plans included "our" writing this book. My heart's desire is that it will touch each reader's heart and encourage him/her in faith.

"Rejoicing always" is impossible in our own strength. We don't always feel joyful, do we? I have learned that joy is a commitment; it is an intentional, conscious decision. We can't always trust our feelings. However, we can trust Jesus. The most important choice we can make is to accept Jesus as our Savior and Lord. Only then will we be able to experience a unique kind of joy which I like to call the "Joy Juice of Jesus."

Some days we need a sip of this juice; other days, we need a gulp or a gallon. Whatever your needs are on that particular day, the joy is ready and waiting for you. You'll soon find that He always gives exactly what you need to fill your heart with the joy of the Lord.

He is the vine; we are the branches (John 15:5). In our garden of life, we should strive to grow His fruit, the fruit of the Spirit. As it blossoms and blooms in our lives, we can drip, drip, drip a little joy here, a little joy there into the lives of those God brings into our path. Sometimes we will be blessed with an abundant crop of joy, and we'll easily and excitedly share it with others. On other days, we may think our joy garden is drying up under the heat of difficult circumstances. But never fear; the Master Gardener is here. He is always busy planting new seeds which will produce the unique fruit of joy from which He squeezes the joy juice that is always perfectly suited for your individual taste. A fresh, new batch is waiting for you. What flavor are you craving today?

"Taste and see that the LORD is good. . ."
Psalm 34:8

Chapter One

Sip the Sweet
Joy Juice
of Jesus

Have you had your Joy Juice today? The flavor called unity is extra sweet and refreshing.

Just as Paul encouraged the Philippians to be "like-minded," we, too, will experience much more joy if we approach life with the spirit of unity (Phil.2:2). So often we do things simply to make a good impression or to please ourselves. Many times this leads to discord, dissension, and disharmony.

Paul wrote in **Philippians 2:3, 4,** *"Do nothing out of selfish ambition or vain conceit, but in humility consider others better than yourselves. Each of you should look not only to your own interests, but also to the interests of others."* Paul was teaching about spiritual unity. We can experience unity if we love one another and are of one spirit and purpose. That means working together, walking in one another's shoes, treating each other's problems as if they were our own. That's what Jesus did, and we are to follow His example. If we will model our lives after Him, we will experience a sweet unity that brings harmony and joy.

So, let's not be so wrapped up in ourselves that we forget to help our friends, acquaintances, or even strangers. Each person God brings into our life is an opportunity to expand our territory of unity and joy.

Prayer: *May I follow Jesus' example. Instead of my selfishness, Lord, make me selfless. Remind me to put others before myself and not expect anything in return. Use me as an agent of unity in my church, at my job place, and with my family. Give me the opportunity to share the joy of Lord wherever I go.*

Have you had your Joy Juice today? Paul must have been drinking a great big glass full when he wrote his letter to the Philippians.

Some might say that Paul's words are irrelevant for us today for they were written so long ago—about AD 61. But the truth is that they're still just as powerful today, especially in this time of uncertainty. Whether it's the rising unemployment rate, the faltering stock market, or the violence throughout the world, there is much that we could focus on that would not be joyful.

But Paul charges us to draw our encouragement from our relationship with Christ and to strive to make our world a better place by having spiritual unity. Listen to what he said in **Philippians 2:1, 2:** ***"If you have any encouragement from being united with Christ, if any comfort from his love, if any fellowship with the Spirit, if any tenderness and compassion, then make my joy complete by being like-minded, having the same love, being one in spirit and purpose."***

Are you working with your co-workers to make sure the job is done well? At church, do you serve with love and unity—even when you don't agree about the color of the carpet? Let's focus on what is truly important, and that's our relationship with Christ. The closer we are to him, the more unified we will be with others, and with unity comes the sweet joy of the Lord.

Prayer: *God, I thank you for the family members and friends that you have brought into my life who are such an encouragement to me. I am blessed to have them, and I appreciate that You lead them to say the things I need to hear just when I need it most. Help me to be that kind of encourager to those around me. Put at least one person in my path today that I can encourage in some way, and give me the wisdom to know who, when, and how. Use me as an instrument of your unity and joy.*

Have you had your Joy Juice today? Slow down, and sip it. Enjoy the sweet natural flavors that were made especially with you in mind.

Do you realize how much joy can be ours just for the asking? God desires to bless each of us with an abundance of joy—so much that we'll be bursting to share a double portion of that joy with others. When you read and study your Bible, you will see the many references to the fruit of joy. The more I study, the more I am convinced that genuine joy is one of the surest signs of the presence of God in a person's life.

Author Bruce Larson says, "If God really is the center of one's life and being, joy is inevitable. If we have no joy, we have missed the heart of the Good News and our bodies, as much as our souls, will suffer the consequences." [1]

Joy is the "enJOYment" of God. We live in such a fast-paced society that days go by and we realize that we haven't even stopped to pray—much less read from God's Word. How can we enjoy a relationship with God if we never take time to be with Him? We all need to slow down for just a few minutes and enjoy being with God today. **Psalm 46:10** reminds us to *"Be still and know that I am God."* It brings

Him great joy when we come into His presence. And it will fill you with joy as well.

Prayer: *Father, it is so hard for me to "be still." I find so many distractions to pull my attention away from simply being with you. Help me to slow down and take time for the most important part of my day—my time spent with you. It touches my heart to think that I can bring joy to You by coming into Your presence. Draw me closer and closer, Lord, so that I may be filled up and ready to share a double portion of Your joy with others.*

Have you had your Joy Juice today? *Be still* so that you won't waste a drop!

"Be still and know that I am God," **Psalm 46:10** says. Many of us find that the only time we're really still is when we're asleep, and we're probably running in our dreams. But being still is an important part of our spiritual growth process. An intimate relationship with God requires quiet time spent alone with God. Church attendance is wonderful and certainly should be a part of every Christian's life, but one-on-one time with Him is how we develop a deep, abiding relationship.

Many years ago when my husband and I were dating, we would spend time together to get to know one another. If we had not been intentional about making that time for one another, we may never have fallen in love. Now, after thirty-seven years of marriage, we enjoy a deep, personal relationship.

I encourage you today to fall in love with Jesus. Be intentional about spending time with Him. *Be still and know that He is God.* You'll soon have that joyful glow about you that can only come from being in love with Him.

Prayer: *Jesus, I do love you, but do my actions show it? Do I demonstrate my love for you by spending time with you on a regular basis? My desire is to continually fall head over heels in love with you. May my love for you grow so deep, so wide, so tall, and so full that joy bursts forth every time I think of you.*

Have you had your Joy Juice today? Do you know Christ well enough to realize that He has made a special batch of sweet Joy Juice just for you?

What's on your agenda today? Do you have a list of meetings, projects, chores, and responsibilities that began racing through your mind just as soon as your feet hit the floor this morning? In the previous devotionals, we've talked about being still. Do you find that as difficult as I do?

In Chuck Swindoll's book *So, You Want to be Like Christ?* he writes, "God will never adjust His agenda to fit ours. He will not speed His pace to catch up with ours; we need to slow our pace in order to recover our walk with Him. God will not scream and shout over the noisy clamor; He expects us to seek quietness, where His still small voice can be heard."[2]

Philippians 3:10 is a wonderful reminder of what the Christian life is all about: *"For my determined purpose is that I may know Him—that I may progressively become more deeply and intimately acquainted with Him"* (AMP). Do you want to know Him in an intimate, deep relationship? Can you hear God's voice amid the hustle and bustle of your busy day? Making time for Christ is imperative for living a life filled with the joy of the Lord.

Prayer: *Yes, Lord, I stay so busy. But I know that I should never be too busy to spend time with you. You are never too busy for me. Place in my heart a desire so enormous and palatable that I will not be able to start my day until I have spent time with You. Give me a hunger and thirst to know You deeply, intimately, and joyfully.*

Have you had your Joy Juice today? What? You don't have time? Slow down just a minute and take the time. You'll be glad you did.

We all have countless duties and responsibilities involving our families, our jobs, and even our churches. We have so many things on our daily calendar that we have to make lists or plug all our activities into our PDAs (personal digital assistants) so that we won't forget anything. Often we are so busy doing good things that we miss God's best.

"Maybe we need to cease some of our activity and hush the noise in our lives so that we can clearly discern what our Father wants to say," writes Priscilla Shirer. She refers to **John 6** where Jesus fed the five thousand: "The people had listened to Jesus teach all day. He realized that they were hungry. In **verse 10** Jesus said, *"Have the people sit down."*" [3]

He distributed the food to those who were *seated*. As Shirer wisely points out, until we take a seat and let go of our frantic activity, He will not fill us. We often miss out on His blessings because we won't just be still.

So, sit down, my friend, and allow God to fill you. He wants to feed you His special recipe for joy.

Prayer: *Here I am, Lord, sitting before you. It may be just a minute or two, but I'm trying to learn to be still. I realize that before you can feed me, I must be seated and ready to accept what you offer. Thank you for speaking to my heart and for slowing me down long enough to seek your face, your grace, and your joy.*

Have you had your Joy Juice today? It will fill you with joyful energy.

There's something invigorating about being around children. They have such joy and such zest for life. They see humor in little things that, so often, we adults miss. I guess, as a general rule, we grownups take ourselves much too seriously.

Jesus enjoyed being with children. Remember His saying, *"Let the little children come to me, and do not hinder them, for the kingdom of heaven belongs to such as these"* (**Matt. 19:14**). I can just imagine him laughing at their cute little jokes and antics. Can't you see Him pulling them onto his lap and listening with interest as they shared what was on their minds. He may have even tickled them to hear their contagious, joyful laughter.

When you're feeling blue, down in the dumps, or just have the "mully grubs" as my mom would say, maybe you should try to be a little more child-like. In other words, stop focusing on the negatives in your life and think cheerful thoughts. **Proverbs 17:22** reminds us that *"A cheerful heart is good medicine, but a crushed spirit dries up the bones."* Now, I don't know about you, but I'll choose a cheerful heart over a crushed spirit and dried up bones any day.

Prayer: *"Jesus loves the little children; all the children of the world. Red and yellow, black and white, they are precious in His sight. Jesus loves the little children of the world."* [4]

Thank you for adopting me into your family, God, and for making me one of Your children.

Have you had your Joy Juice today? Your parents would encourage you to drink every drop.

As I grow older, I realize how blessed I was to have godly parents who loved me and my siblings unconditionally. Now, that didn't mean that they were always pleased with our actions or the decisions we made. We did embarrass them often with some of our shenanigans. But, they always forgave us because they loved us unconditionally. What an example of the love of Christ! If you have Godly parents, stop right now and thank God for them. If not, then pray for them to receive Christ. If they have passed on, pray that God will show you how to be an example of His unconditional love to those He has put under your influence.

Because of our human nature, we make decisions that are not always pleasing to our Heavenly Father. I'm sure He is disappointed often. But, He is always willing to forgive us if we will come before Him with a repentant heart.

God doesn't expect perfection. Remember that He made us. Don't pull away from Him because of the choices you've made in the past. Give it all to Him today, and accept His love and forgiveness. When you do this, your life will be filled with a joy and a *"peace that passes all understanding"* as **Philippians 4:7** so beautifully reminds us.

Prayer: Dear *Father God, Abba, I love to feel Your loving arms around me. Pull me into Your sweet embrace today as You whisper Your Word into my heart. Cover me in Your peace and protection and remind me to demonstrate Your unconditional love.*

Have you had your Joy Juice today? Even grand-parents need Joy Juice.

One of the glorious things about growing older is having grandchildren. Talk about joy! Those of you who have arrived at this station of life know exactly what I mean. Papa Pat and I look forward to our grands' visits, and we count it a privilege to answer their zillion questions: "What ya doing?" "Can I help?" "Wanna hear the song I made up?" "Do fish have houses?" "Can butterflies talk?"

Most grandparents will admit that when we were raising our own children, many days we didn't think we had the time really to enjoy the little pleasures. But with age comes the experience that proves just how quickly time passes. The Bible is correct when it states that life is a mist, a vapor (James 4:14).

Young parents, it's true that your days are so busy right now with the rearing of your family. But don't lose sight of the fact that the time you have with your children is fleeting. Each child is a blessing from above. **Psalm 127:3** reminds us accordingly: *"Sons are a heritage from the LORD, children a reward from him."*

So, Moms, as you wash that third washer of clothes today, and Dads, when you stub your toe on that toy that was left in the middle of the floor, remember the *"joy of the Lord is our strength"* (Nehemiah 8:10)—even in child-rearing.

Prayer: *Dear Lord, it is with a humble heart that I accept your gracious invitation and opportunity to help mold a child's life. Please help me not only to teach about You with words, but help me to live such a Godly life before him/her that what I do speaks more loudly that what I say. Make my life the role model for joy.*

Have you had your Joy Juice today? I said Joy Juice, not happy juice.

Often we get joy confused with happiness. Everyone wants to be happy and if we're not careful, we fall into the trap of chasing this dream of perfection. Let's think about the difference between joy and happiness. Simply put, *happiness* depends on what's *happening* in our lives. If the circumstances around us are great and everything seems to be going our way, then we're happy. But then, when the tide turns and things start happening that we'd not planned, when challenges arise that upset us and unexpected hurts occur, we lose our happiness.

The NIV Life Application Bible explains the difference in these two terms: "In contrast to happiness stands joy. Running deeper and stronger, joy is the quiet, confident assurance of God's love and work in our lives—that He will be there no matter what! Happiness depends on happenings, but joy depends on Christ." [5]

When we pray, let's ask God to pour out the sweet joy of the Lord in our lives. **1 Thessalonians 5:16** instructs us to *"Be joyful always"*. That doesn't mean that every day will be a happy day, but if we have a personal relationship with the Sweet Joy-Giver, then joy can always be ours.

Prayer: *What a friend I have in you, Jesus! Thank you for going ahead of me, walking beside me, and following after me. Knowing that you are always with me fills my heart with joy.*

Have you had your Joy Juice today? I promise, if you drink the genuine juice, you'll have the joy of the Lord.

Be reminded that joy is not always a happy feeling. Just because we are believers doesn't mean that our lives will always be wonderful and full of sunshine each and every day. God makes many promises, but he never said that we will be free from trials and tough times.

Have you noticed that when you're really trying to walk the Christian walk and you're striving to fulfill God's purpose for your life, it seems the enemy works overtime? Things are moving along smoothly and then—out of nowhere—whammo! You get hit right between the eyes with something that you weren't expecting. This is how Satan tries to discourage and defeat us.

But we know the One Who is stronger and mightier; He loves us more than words can express. Our Father wants us to trust in Him—especially when times are tough.

"Consider it pure joy," says **James 1:2, *"whenever you face trials of many kinds."*** James didn't say we'll be happy during these tough times, but because

of our relationship with Christ, we can experience joy.

As you face the world today, be joyful in the truth that we can expect to experience joy—even in the trials. We are being pruned and polished into one of God's beautiful masterpieces, a creation of joy.

Prayer: *Dear Precious Heavenly Father, hold my hand, lift me up, and give me security. Fill me with your strength when I feel I cannot go on; fill me with your power when I am weak; give me your comfort when I hurt. Turn my weeping into joy.*

Have you had your Joy Juice today? When we are intentional about sharing the joy of the Lord, that Joy Juice is delicious.

I guess you've noticed that I love to talk about joy. I believe that the more we talk about something, the more intentional we become about making it a goal. Who couldn't use more joy in their life—especially joy from the Lord?

Joy is a healer. **Proverbs 17:22** reminds us that ***"A joyful heart is good medicine, but a crushed spirit dries up the bones"*** **(ESV)**. Many times a happy heart leads to laughter. Doctors tell us that laughter has many benefits:

- It reduces stress and tension.
- It strengthens our immune system.
- It's great exercise for our lungs.
- It increases circulation.
- It even reduces pain.

God created us with a need for joy and laughter. Can you remember the last time you had a good belly laugh? If you can't, you need some serious Joy Juice. Find some good friends who love to laugh and hang out with them for a while. Try to see the humor in your circumstances, and laugh at yourself. If all else fails, find some children to keep you company. Volunteer at school or church in the children's department, and I can assure you that before you know it, your funny bone will be struck with joy.

Look for reasons to laugh. God delights when His children are joyful. And joy is contagious. Be infectious today.

Prayer: *Just thinking of You brings a smile to my face, Father. Thank you for creating laughter, and remind me to use this gift often. Give me a joyful heart and opportunities to share laughter, giggles, snickers, and guffaws with friends and family.*

Chapter Two

Fresh and Fruity
Joy Juice

Have you had your Joy Juice today? It's very healthy for you because it's made with genuine fruit from the true vine (John 15:1).

In order to assure that you are eating healthy, you should be sure to include fruit in your daily diet. Nutritionists tell us that we need between five and nine servings per day. Fruit is 100% bad-cholesterol free. It's stimulates the memory; it has healing effects. There are many reasons that eating fruit makes us feel better physically.

Did you know that the Bible talks about fruit, too? In **Galatians 5: 22, 23** we read, *"But the fruit of the Spirit is love, joy, peace, patience, kindness, goodness, faithfulness, gentleness and self-control."* If we want to grow healthy spiritually, we need to ask God to help us apply each of these nine servings of fruit each and every day.

"The fruit of the Spirit refers to the spontaneous work of the Holy Spirit in us. The Spirit produces these character traits that are found in the nature of Christ. When this fruit is evident in our lives, it's only because they are the by-products of Christ's control in us." [1] We can't gather this kind of fruit by ourselves. We must depend on God's help to plant, cultivate, and harvest this fruit.

Why not ask God to plant a fruit garden in your heart? You might just find yourself with so much fruit that you'll be making Joy Juice to share with your neighbors.

Prayer: *Dear God, I ask for the Fruit of the Spirit to sprout, bud, and bloom in my life. Help me to remember that a good garden takes a lot of cultivating, but I do not have to tend the garden alone. I can always trust that the Master Gardener will be there to help me.*

Have you had your Joy Juice today? Do you like the flavor today? It's made from real fruit.

We all know how important it is to make sure that fruit is a part of our diet. It's good for us physically, as well as spiritually. Let's take a close look at **Galatians 5** to understand what kind of fruit we need for our spiritual health.

The first fruit mentioned in **verse 22** is the fruit of love. It's not an accident that this fruit is first on the list. If we don't have love, our Christian example will be ineffective. As my Bible footnote explains: "Love is more important than all the spiritual gifts exercised in the church body. Great acts of faith, acts of dedication or sacrifice produce very little without love. Love makes our actions and gifts useful." [2]

The way I see it, we have to accept God's love in order to be able to give it away. God's love is directed outward—toward others. It is possible to practice this kind of love only if God helps us set aside our own desires and instincts. Only then can we give love while expecting nothing in return. The more we become like Christ, the more love we will show to others. That's why one of our most passionate heart's desires should be to be like Christ. Meditate and pray over the scripture found in **Galatians 5:22, 23**. With

God's help, you can be a joyful Christian who radiates the love of Christ.

Prayer: *Loving Heavenly Father, first I must thank you for your love for me. I am so undeserving. Yet, because of Your unconditional love, I can live an abundant life of joy. Help me to show Your love to others as I go along my way today and every day. Love through me.*

Have you had your Joy Juice today? This chapter's batch of Joy Juice has a fruity flavor. Have you noticed?

We've been discussing the fruit of the Spirit found in **Galatians 5.** The first fruit on the list is love. Then comes joy. Paul teaches that if we want the fruit of the Spirit to grow in us, we must join our lives to God. In **John 15:4** Jesus tells us, ***"Remain in me, and I will remain in you. No branch can bear fruit by itself; it must remain in the vine. Neither can you bear fruit unless you remain in me."***

So, if we want a life filled with joy, we must remain in Him every moment of the day. Genuine joy comes from the fruit garden that is deep within the heart of one who has surrendered his all to Christ. Sure, life is going to serve up some sour crops from time to time. Our fruit cobbler might not always be tasty and sweet, but we can always wash it down with lots of joy juice.

We know that the Master Chef has our best interests in mind. He knows what we need to help us develop and grow spiritually. Next time life serves you something bitter or distasteful, ask the Master what you can learn from the experience. If you are remaining in Him, you will be able to face whatever it is with a special recipe of joy.

Prayer: *Dear Lord, help me to remain in you. I can't bear the right kind of fruit without Your help. Please cook up a delicious recipe of joy in me and remind me to share that joy with others.*

Have you had your Joy Juice today? What kind of fruit have you chosen to enjoy with your Joy Juice snack?

We've been talking about the fruit of the Spirit in our last few devotionals. We learned that the fruit of love is of utmost importance; then there's joy that we certainly want to share with others. What's next on the list in **Galatians 5:22**? It's the fruit of peace.

In one of David Jeremiah's online devotionals he told this story:

Two artists were asked to paint pictures of peace as they perceived it. One painted a quiet, still lake, far back in the mountains. The other painted a raging, rushing waterfall which had a birch tree leaning out over it with a bird resting in a nest on one of the branches. Which one truly depicts peace? The second one does, because there is no such thing as peace without opposition. The first picture may look serene and is a beautiful scene. But it doesn't depict God's rest. His peace is a spiritual peace, one that operates in the midst of the storm. Jesus didn't come to remove all our problems, but instead to give us a different approach to the storms of life. [3]

What's your approach to the difficulties of life? Do you fret and worry? Do you try to handle things in your own strength? Sometimes we just feel like pulling the covers over our heads and staying in bed, never facing our problems at all. But always remember: we don't have to handle it by ourselves. We've got a friend, and His name is Jesus.

Though we do not know what storms may be ahead, we can be assured that the peace of God can be ours—no matter what. Love, joy, peace—delicious fruit. Enjoy them each and every day.

Prayer: *Dear Father God, only You know what the future holds. Help me not to worry and fret; instead, help me to put my total trust in you. Hold my hand, Lord, through every circumstance, and give me wisdom to make godly decisions. Flavor my joy juice with peace.*

Have you had your Joy Juice today? We've had a steady diet of fruit for the past few days. **Galatians 5** has taught us about the fruit of the Spirit: love, joy, peace. The next one on the list is patience.

Many times I feel like uttering a desperate prayer to God: "Lord, give me patience and give it to me quick!" In my own strength, I don't always do so well in this area. Patience is a fruit of the Spirit, and that means it's something God does in us. But, we must cooperate with Him.

For example, when someone annoys or hurts us, we need to pull out the fruit of love and take a great big bite. If we're stuck behind that pokey driver, instead of aggressively tailgating, let's chew on that fruit and try to imagine the driver as someone we love—maybe our grandparents. You don't tailgate your grandparents; you protect them.

To put it another way, try to see difficult people the way Jesus sees them. We wonder why they're acting in such an obnoxious way or why they are so distant or arrogant. It could be because of tremendous pain in their lives. Maybe they've been hurt, and they're trying to protect themselves. When we allow God to develop that fruit called patience in our lives, we begin to see things from a whole different perspective—one that is flavored with His love, His joy, His peace, and His patience.

Prayer: *Oh, Father, how thankful I am that you are patient with me. Please take my impatience, my irritability, and my judgmental attitude; replace them with your patience, your kindness, and your unconditional love.*

Have you had your Joy Juice today? It's certainly a healthy drink. Not only is it good for your spiritual health, but it affects your emotional and physical health as well.

Many of us are striving toward becoming healthier. That involves making better choices. We've talked about adding fruit to our spiritual diet—the fruit of the Spirit. Galatians 5: 22, 23 names a variety of fruit that we should have as we mature in our Christian walk. We've talked about love, joy, peace, and patience. The next fruit listed in that passage is kindness.

One of the first Bible verses many of us learned as children was *"And be ye kind one to another"* (**Eph. 4:32**, KJV). It was easy to recite but not so easy to live out. Let's look at that verse a little more closely. The NIV says it this way: *"Be kind and compassionate to one another, forgiving each other, just as in Christ God forgave you."* Have you noticed how often the Bible links being kind with forgiving others? It's easy to be kind to those who are kind to us. But what about those who are spiteful and seem to try to hurt us? **Luke 6:28** has the answer for that: *"Bless those who curse you, pray for those who mistreat you."*

If we desire to be like Christ, kindness is a necessary fruit. Share this fruit with everyone. You'll be surprised how much more joyful you will be.

Prayer: *Kind and loving God, give me a forgiving heart. Remind me daily of Your forgiveness of my sins. Develop in me each fruit of the Spirit so that I may become more and more like You each day. Give me an opportunity today to show kindness.*

Have you had your Joy Juice today? Haven't you enjoyed tasting that good fruit of love, joy, peace, patience, and kindness that we've been sampling from Galatians 5? What's on the fruit platter for today? It's goodness.

We use the word *good* many times a day. To praise a child, we say, "Good job!" We tell one another when we've seen a good movie or read a good book or found a good restaurant. But what does goodness mean in the spiritual context?

James Hamilton wrote, "Goodness is love in action, love with its hand to the plow, love with the burden on its back, love following His footsteps Who went about continually doing good."[4] That's exactly what Jesus did; He went about doing good as we are reminded in **Acts 10:38**. Can we do that? Yes, *if* we are walking with Him.

"The fruit of the Spirit must continually be cultivated," writes Roger Cotton, "We don't produce it once for all time. It's a continual process of becoming more like Him so that goodness will be expressed in our lives instead of the old, selfish qualities. If we focus on the wrong things, we will reap some very selfish, evil fruit in our behavior and relationships. But when we meditate on God's qualities, we bear good fruit which leads to kind, generous, loving acts toward others." [5]

Start sharing the fruit of goodness, and before you know it, you'll be spreading the joy of the Lord in all kinds of ways and in all kinds of places.

Prayer: *Father, I am continually in awe of Your goodness. Help me to be more like You. Make me selfless and more compassionate to those around me. I so desire to have the fruit of goodness in my life, but I realize that I often fail to exhibit it. Give me the perseverance to never give up because developing the fruit of the Spirit is a process, a continual process.*

Have you had your Joy Juice today? Fruity Juice has been our focus the past several days. Are you feeling healthier by drinking it faithfully?

The fruit of the Spirit is something that all Christians should desire as a part of their daily spiritual diet. The fruit on our menu for today is faithfulness—such an important quality.

In **1 Corinthians 16:13,** Paul teaches that we should "*stand firm in the faith.*" This admonition means that we should not get discouraged or give up easily. If we have faith in God, then we can be strong because faith gives us the ground on which to stand. Standing firm, being faithful in even the little things, is imperative to becoming spiritually mature.

Many of us are not faithful in the little things. We sometimes break our promises, don't follow through on an obligation, or don't show up for engagements. Some people fail to pay their debts promptly. How can we demonstrate faithfulness in all things? We can start by being on time for work or appointments. We can make that phone call to the person whom God has laid on our heart, and especially, we can faithfully spend time with Him. As Rev. James R. Miller writes, "The person who is always dependable, who is faithful in the least, as well as in the greatest, whose life and character are true through and through, gives out a light in this world which honors Christ and blesses [brings joy to] others." [6]

Prayer: *Great is thy faithfulness! Let this be the song of my heart, dear God. May I be constantly reminded that Your mercies are new every day. Draw me closer and closer to You so that I might be a model of faithfulness on earth for my Father, who is in Heaven. Help me to be faithful in all things, small and large; minor and major; private and public. May I faithfully exude Your* joy.

Have you had your Joy Juice today? We've tasted lots of fruit these past few days, but here's another delicious one we need to try—gentleness.

Jesus is the perfect example. In **Matthew 11:29**, He said, *"Take my yoke upon you and learn from me, for I am gentle and humble in heart, and you will find rest for your souls."* For the word gentleness, some versions of the Bible use the word meekness, but this is not to be confused with weakness. Gentleness describes a calm disposition, particularly under fire—which actually requires a great deal of strength.

There is a story told of George Washington that demonstrates biblical meekness or gentleness. "On one occasion, he was fox hunting with a group of friends. One of the fields through which they were passing was bordered by a stone wall. As his horse jumped the wall, it knocked off a stone. Washington immediately got down from his horse, and replaced the stone. One of his friends said, "You are too big a man to bother with that." He replied, "No, I am just the right size." [7]

Gentleness includes true humility that does not consider itself too good or too exalted for humble tasks. Next time you are tempted to think, "Someone else should do that," ask yourself if you are exhibiting the attitude of gentleness. Jesus did.

Joyfully accept your opportunities to bear this wonderful fruit.

Prayer: *Dear Jesus, You are such a model for meekness. Remind me that it is not a sign of weakness to be gentle and meek—just the opposite. Give me the strength and humility to face each day with the meekness of Christ. Put me on the road to a joyful journey.*

Have you had your Joy Juice today? I've got one more fruit that I want you to try today. This one may not be as tasty as the others. It's the fruit of self-control.

Self-control, or temperance, simply means to have the strength to control the self. We know this is not possible until we surrender totally to Christ. This last fruit on the list in Galatians 5 makes all the other fruit operative. Ask yourself: Do I exhibit self-control in my daily walk?

The Bible gives us instruction:

- 2 Corinthians 10:5 reminds us that we are to keep control of our thoughts, taking every thought captive.
- James 3 tells us to guard our tongues. We are told explicitly not to lie, bear false witness, or gossip.
- James 4 instructs us to avoid sinning in our relationships with others.

These are just some of the ways God instructs us to use self-control. And He knows that we need His help. If we will allow Him, the Holy Spirit will work in our hearts to help us live above sinful practices.

As a result, we can model God's values and apply those values to our actions and reactions. We must depend on His power to help us daily so that we can more effectively share His love for others and spread His joy.

Prayer: *Dear Lord, I invite You to be the LORD of my life. Help me to take myself off the throne and relinquish control to You. I realize that only when I'm God-controlled will I develop the fruit of self-control. I give You today; please guide me to do only Your will.*

Chapter Three

Luscious Joy Juice:
The
Libation of
Love

Have you had your Joy Juice today? February 14th is known to the world as the day of love. If you need a gift idea this year for your special Valentine, may I suggest a delicious bottle of Joy Juice?

One of the favorite days of the whole year for primary and elementary school children is Valentine's Day. I vividly remember how thrilled I was as a child when the exciting month of February arrived. We could not wait until our teachers had art time and let us make our Valentine box or envelope. What anticipation to see who would drop a card in your holder! And though each paper Valentine said about the same thing, if that special person gave you a Valentine card, you could read between the lines and make it say something extra special.

Did you know that each of us has our very own Valentine holder that we can look into every day of the year? It called the Holy Bible. It is filled with love notes and expressions of affection, intended especially for you. You don't have to read between the lines because God makes it crystal clear that you are loved. You were loved so much that He sent his one and only Son to die for you.

John 3:16 never gets old: *"For God so loved the world that he gave his one and only Son, that* *whoever believes in him shall not perish but have eternal life.*" If you were the only person on earth, God still would have sent His son for you. Now, that's love—an amazing, indescribable love—that should fill your heart with joy.

Prayer: *My precious, Lord, I love you for loving me. Even before I was born, you knew me and loved me. And then to send Your Son, Your one and only Son to die for me. I just cannot fathom that kind of love. Your sacrificial love brings joy to my life. Help me to show Your love and joy to others.*

Have you had your Joy Juice today? Share with others to demonstrate Christ's love and joy.

Even if you don't have a romantic sweetheart, you can still think of those who need an expression of God's love. As a matter of fact, I'd like to encourage you to think of someone who may seldom hear the words "I love you." It may be a person who has lost a mate, a friend who is going through a divorce, or that person who doesn't make friends easily. No matter what our age or what our circumstances may be, we all need to feel loved. And the Bible exhorts us to *"love one another. As I have loved you, so you must love one another"* **(John 13:34).**

Acts of love don't have to cost money. They can be very inexpensive. For instance, pick up the telephone or drop by for a short visit and express your appreciation for that person's friendship/relationship. Your love gift may be something as simple as a hug or a handshake, accompanied by a genuine smile and word of encouragement. And who doesn't enjoy getting a handwritten note filled with edifying words?

Author and lecturer, Leo Buscaglia told the story of one four year old boy who went to visit his next door neighbor. "The elderly gentleman had just lost his wife in death and he was crying. The mother watched as her little boy climbed onto the neighbor's lap and sat there, silently, for several minutes. When he returned to his mother, she asked him what he was doing. 'Helping him cry,' was the little boy's answer." [1]

You see, sometimes we can express our love in the simplest of acts. Just a few minutes of our time and kindness can be all it takes to share the love and joy of the Lord with others.

Prayer: *Lead me, Lord, to the person in my life today that needs that extra expression of love; then show me how to express Your love in a way that he/she will best understand it.*

Have you had your Joy Juice today? I hope you've been thinking about how to share your Joy Juice with others so they will feel God's love through you.

Today, I'd like to encourage you to talk with the children and young people in your life over whom you have influence. Go ahead and prepare them for Valentine's Day. You know how excited they will be over getting cards and candy from their friends. Talk with them about what they can give this Valentine's Day, instead of focusing on what they are going to get.

Acts 20:35 reminds us: *"**Remembering the words the Lord Jesus himself said: 'It is more blessed to give than to receive'.**"* Ask the children, "Do you know that you can give things that don't cost any money?" Then, give them some suggestions:

- You can give your parents a hug and an "I love you." That affection would mean more to them than anything you could buy.
- You can call or visit your grandparents and/or draw them a picture. Just to know that you took the time out of your busy day to think of them is such a nice gift.

- You can be obedient and use your manners at school. Your teacher would be so grateful for a day when she didn't have to remind any of her students of the rules.

- Think of that person who doesn't have many friends. Invite him or her to play with you at recess or sit with you at lunch. Everyone needs a friend, and you may never know how much that simple act could mean to someone.

Encourage your young friends to think of other ways to share the love of Jesus with others. Remind them that they don't have to wait until Valentine's Day. They can start today and make a joyful difference in someone's life.

Prayer: *Lord Jesus, I smile as I think of how often You expressed love and interest in little children. Show me some young person today that needs some guidance about showing love to others. Let me use this opportunity to teach them about You and how to have the joy of the Lord by inviting You into their heart and by sharing Your love with others.*

Have you had your Joy Juice today? One of the most important ingredients in the Joy Juice recipe is love.

In **John 15:9**, Jesus teaches his disciples: *"As the Father has loved me, so have I loved you. Now remain in my love."* In this passage, *Father* refers to God. We all can glean truth from this verse that applies to our lives. Our Father loves us. And as His child, we are to pass that love along to others as we remain in His love. Let's think about how we can best show the love of our Heavenly Father to our children, grandchildren, and all those young people in our lives. We should always strive to be a godly example of love to those who are looking to us for a role model.

Let's do a personal love check. Do we exhibit Godly characteristics that teach our children how they should "love the Lord with all their heart, soul, and mind" (Matt. 22:37)? Do we "love our neighbor as ourselves" (Matt. 9:19) or does our example teach that we should always put *ourselves* first? Are we "slow to anger" (Psalm 103:8)? Do we "do to others as we would have them do to us" (Luke 6:31)? Are the words that come from our mouths words of love that "build others up according to their need" (Eph.

4:29)? Are we "kind, compassionate, and forgiving" (Eph. 4:32)? Ask God to remove any blinders from your eyes and show you what kind of example you are setting.

You might be thinking, "Whew! I'm off the hook! I don't have any children." Sorry…but each of us needs to be accountable. Every one of us has younger ones looking to us for an example, whether they are relatives or not. Please be aware that you are a person of influence in someone's life. Pray that the Lord will enable you to show His love and joy on a daily basis.

Prayer: *Father of Love, I realize that young ones are watching my actions, listening to my words and learning by observing my life. Help me to be keenly aware of this as I strive to be more like you. Fill my heart with the desire to be a godly role model for all those you have put in my life, regardless of their age. In you, Lord, may I find joy and may that joy be contagious.*

Have you had your Joy Juice today? Bring joy to your special sweetheart today by sharing your Joy Juice with him/her.

When we talk about a sweetheart, who comes to your mind? A boyfriend or girlfriend? A child or grandchild? A really special friend? For those of you who are married, I hope you immediately thought of your husband or wife.

Married couples, please remember that your spouse is God's provision for you. The Bible tells us, ***"Husbands, love your wives, just as Christ loved the church and gave himself up for her"*** **(Eph. 5:25).** We're also reminded in that same book that we should ***"submit to one another out of reverence for Christ"*** **(Eph. 5:21).** Don't wait for Valentine's Day to show your love. Your mate needs to hear words of love and commitment continually. Tell your mate often that he/she is your sweetheart. We all love to hear the words that indicate that we are special. Occasionally, write it down for him/her to read over and over again. That's a very inexpensive gift but one of great value. And the best thing of all is that it will bring joy to both of you.

For those who are not married, know that God has a plan for you, too. Be ready to share His love with those He brings into your path. Pray and ask God to make you aware of those who really need that pat on the back or that word of encouragement. Someone may need you simply to listen or to send them a brief note letting them know that you are thinking of them. All these gestures are expressions of love. God's love is big enough to cover all. And the exciting news is that when you share His love with others, your own heart is filled with joy.

Prayer: *Precious Jesus, loving Savior, I thank You for Your provision in my life. Please accept my gratitude for those You have given me that I can call family and friends. May my love shine forth today as a beacon of Your light and love so that I will bring Your joy to others.*

Have you had your Joy Juice today? When you drink a healthy portion, you'll find that you are filled with a renewed sense of God's love and strength.

Isn't it such a comfort and a joy booster to know that God loves you? You do know that, don't you? Listen to the words in **1 John 3:1**: *"How great is the love the Father has lavished on us, that we should be called children of God!"* When you accept Jesus into your heart and life, you are His child, and He desires to lavish His love on you.

That doesn't mean that everything is going to be perfect in our lives. We will still have tough times. But through those challenges, we can feel His love being poured out on us. Sometimes it's simply in the peace He gives in the midst of the storm; other times, He gives us a miracle. Often it's His constant, abiding love—simply knowing that *"The Lord is near"* (**Psalm 145:18**).

All of us have been affected by our nation's economic condition, but may I suggest that there are positive things coming from this seemingly dismal picture? People are coming to the aid of others and are sharing what they have with those who don't have. More importantly, many of us are praying more fervently and faithfully. Everything is in His hands, and because of His unending love for us, His children, we can rest and trust in Him.

Keep that bottle of Joy Juice handy. You never know when you'll need to share with someone who needs a reminder of God's loving kindness.

Prayer: *Almighty, loving God. I love the feeling of your arms around me. Nothing can take the place of the security of knowing that You are looking out for me. I do feel lavished in Your love, and that fills me with* joy.

Have you had your Joy Juice today? I love to drink mine. How 'bout you?

Speaking of love, who has a special place in your heart? A spouse, your parents, your children or grandchildren, a dear friend? Sometimes we are so full of love for a person that we feel like shouting it from the mountain top.

Parents, think about the day your child was born. You bubbled with excitement. You loved that baby the instant he/she was born (and even before). You couldn't keep that love a secret.

We *say* we love Jesus, but how often do we tell others about our love for Him? Have you ever been in a group when someone brings up the subject of Jesus? Often it gets quiet and uncomfortable. Why? Are we ashamed?

Jesus said, ***"If anyone is ashamed of me and my words in this adulterous and sinful generation, the Son of Man will be ashamed of him when he comes in his Father's glory with the holy angels"*** (**Mark 8:38**). When we see Jesus face to face, do we want Him to be ashamed of us? Or do we want Him to open His arms wide, recognizing us as a part of His family and hear Him say, ***"Well done, good and faithful servant"*** (**Matt. 25:21**)?

Tell others of your love for Him today. Don't ever be ashamed to proclaim your love for the One who can fill your life with joy from now throughout eternity.

Prayer: *Father, I confess that many times I don't speak up and tell others about You. Please fill me with Your boldness so that I will never be ashamed to share Your love and joy with others.*

Have you had your Joy Juice today? Why don't you give a bottle to a friend as a gift of love?

That's one of the ways God expresses his love for us. He continually gives us gifts. **James 1:17** says, ***"Every good and perfect gift is from above, coming down from the Father of the heavenly lights, who does not change like shifting shadows."***

In Gary Chapman's book *The Five Love Languages,* he says that some of us speak our love with "words of affirmation;" others by sharing "quality time." Still others speak the language of "service" or "physical touch." But the Love Language I'd like for us to consider today is the language of "gifts." [2]

God speaks all five of these love languages because He knows that all of us need different expressions to understand His love for us. The language of gifts, however, is one He speaks exceptionally well. He is fluent in this language. Just think about it: He gives us the air that we breathe, the food that we eat, and our five senses to enjoy His creation. He gives us material possessions, friends, and family. If we tried to list all His gifts, we would run out of pages. He is such a generous and loving God.

Today, I'd like to challenge you to be God's mouthpiece through which He can speak His language of love. Share His love every chance you get. The more you give, the more joyful you will be, and then you'll have more Joy Juice to share with others.

Prayer: *You speak love in all languages, Father God. You are always fluent in the language I understand and are so willing to speak to me when I need it the most. Thank you for all the gifts that you so generously pour into, onto, and throughout my life.*

Have you had your Joy Juice today? Look at the label on your bottle of juice this morning. It says, "Made with love, especially for you."

God is such a generous God. He has poured out His blessings on us in countless ways. One of God's many expressions of love is His written Word, the Holy Bible. Within the pages of this beautiful book, we find reminder after reminder of His love for us. It's as if He has compiled a treasure chest of love letters, written especially for you and me. Have you read them lately?

Look at this verse from **Psalm 36:7**: *"How precious is Your steadfast love, O God! The children of men take refuge and put their trust under the shadow of Your wings" (AMP)*. Because of His love for us, His steadfast love, we can always trust Him, regardless of our circumstances. Whether it's the loss of a job, sickness, death of a loved one, or when it looks as if everyone has deserted us, God is still with us. And God is love. **1 John 4:16** reminds us of this truth: *"God is love, and he who abides in love abides in God, and God in him" (NKJV)*.

Sit back and relax with your bottle of special-made Joy Juice. Bask in the warmth of His love. It will fill you with that glorious joy of the Lord.

Prayer: *"How precious is Your steadfast love, O God!" Help me to abide in You every minute of every day.*

Have you had your Joy Juice today? Show your love by giving some away. You'll be surprised how joyful you will be.

"Your attitude should be the same as that of Christ Jesus," we are instructed in **Philippians 2:5**. He didn't come to earth to *be* served but to serve and to give His life. Now, that's love! Are you willing to fulfill God's plan by serving and giving in the ways he leads you? One of the best demonstrations of the love of God working in and through us is to serve others. Since serving doesn't come naturally to us, we should ask God to give us a servant's heart.

A willing servant serves joyfully. He/she has a heart attitude of love for the Lord and is, therefore, willing to serve with the attitude of Christ. Are you serving with a smile or a scowl? Remember, it's all in the attitude. When we are seeking God's plan for our lives, He will guide us to the acts of service He has planned for us. In order to be filled with the joy of the Lord, we must empty ourselves of selfish attitudes, pride, and anything that distracts us from Him.

Rick Warren uses the old comparison between the Sea of Galilee and the Dead Sea: "Galilee is a lake full of life because it takes in water but also gives it out. In contrast, nothing lives in the Dead Sea because, with no outflow, the lake has stagnated." [3]

Are you a Sea of Galilee or a Dead Sea? If we take, take, take and never give, then we're going to be a Dead Sea—never fulfilling God's plan for our lives. In contrast, when we take in the things of the Lord by studying His Word and growing in our relationship with Him, we'll be a joyful Sea of Galilee, overflowing our banks with His love as we spill out into the lives of others.

Prayer: *Father, I want to be a Sea of Galilee. Please remove the selfish scales from my eyes so that I can see the needs of others. Give me a servant's heart, the attitude of Jesus, and joy beyond containment.*

Chapter Four

Bitter Made Better

Have you had your Joy Juice today? As I was reading my Bible and sipping my Joy Juice a few mornings ago, I came across the passage of scripture in Ephesians that says, *"Do not let any unwholesome talk come out of your mouths, but only what is helpful for building others up according to their needs, that it may benefit those who listen"* **(Eph. 4:9).**

I began to think back over my life at all the times that I had miserably failed in this area. Those times when I lost my cool with my children and said things that were not "helpful in building them up." I thought of all the times when I carelessly passed on gossip without even considering whom it might hurt and the occasions when my words were judgmental and critical of others. Ever been there?

How can we be sure that the words that come out of our mouths are wholesome? We should start by repenting. We've all fallen short in this area. Then we need to allow God to be in control of our thoughts, our reactions, and our words. Before we open our mouths, we should ask ourselves the following questions: "Would Jesus say this?" "Are my words going to be helpful in building this person up?" "Will the people who hear my words benefit as they listen?"

If the answer to any of these questions is no, then we need to simply be quiet until God fills our mouth with His words—words that will bring joy to those who will hear.

Prayer: *Oh, Father, how many times have I misused the gift of speech to hurt people rather than edify them? Please make me sensitive to others and let me aim to make my words sweet and encouraging. Remind me continually that once the words are out of my mouth, I can never take them back. Fill my heart with love and joy so that my words will indicate that you are in control of my life.*

Have you had your Joy Juice today? Ephesians 4:29 talks about not letting unwholesome talk come out of our mouths. That's one good way to serve Joy Juice to those around us.

Do you realize what happens when we don't allow God total control of our thoughts and tongues? Our words most likely will become UNwholesome. **Ephesians 4:30** says, *"And do not grieve the Holy Spirit of God."* Oh, my! Does this mean that when we allow hurtful words, critical remarks, or angry retorts to spew from our lips that we have grieved the Holy Spirit? I'm afraid that is exactly what it means.

I researched what *grieved* means in the context of this scripture. "The word denotes a pain or grief that can only be experienced between two people who deeply love each other." [1] This tells us that the relationship that exists between us and the Holy Spirit is inexpressibly precious. The Holy Spirit is deeply in love with us. Are we in love with Him? We need to realize how special the Holy Spirit is in our lives and to honor Him by making sure that we live wholesome, upright, holy lives.

A holy life includes the words that come from our mouths, the attitudes we have toward each other and our behavior on a day to day basis. Let's bring joy to the Holy Spirit rather than grieving Him. When we commit to doing this, joy will be a part of our lives.

Prayer: *Father, I do not intentionally set out to grieve You, but I know that many times I do. Please guard and guide my thoughts, my words, and my actions. Help me to live according to Your instructions. Give me a hunger and thirst to stay in the Word. I want Your scriptures to be such a part of me that I will instinctively act in godly wisdom. I desire to bring You joy, Father.*

Have you had your Joy Juice today? No matter what flavor, Joy Juice will make the bitter much better.

Ephesians 4 is a power-packed chapter of instruction for those who want to become more like Christ and spread His joy. Look at **4:31**: *"Get rid of all bitterness, rage and anger, brawling and slander, along with every form of malice."*

Wow! That's a tall order. Paul first mentions bitterness. When a person becomes offended and doesn't deal with that offense correctly, it becomes embedded in the heart and soul. Then, it turns into bitterness. If we're not careful, we can become so inwardly infected with bitterness that we are outwardly affected in our appearance and disposition. Then comes the rage, anger, slander, and maybe even brawling to which the scripture refers.

It's time for a self-check. If you find yourself constantly saying negative things about someone who has offended you or upset you in the past, it may be that a root of bitterness is trying to grow inside your heart. Call the Master Surgeon and genuinely repent before Him. Then ask Him to rip those destructive roots clear out of your soul. If you don't, the root of bitterness will go down deep into the soil of your soul, and eventually you will be filled with bitter fruit. And do you know who that hurts most? It hurts you as well as those over whom you have influence. Not only that, it will also steal your joy.

Prayer: *God, please replace any bitter fruit in my life with your sweet, joyful fruit. Point out any root that is trying to take hold in my heart and sever it before it goes deep. I want my heart to be filled with the joy of the Lord; only you can plant the right seeds, nurture them, and make them grow into something beautiful in my life.*

Have you had your Joy Juice today? I hope it's sweet, instead of the bitter kind that we talked about yesterday.

Continuing our study of **Ephesians 4**, let's look at verse **32** today: *"Be kind and compassionate to one another, forgiving each other, just as in Christ God forgave you."* Most of would say that we try to be kind to others. But it is really difficult to be kind to someone who has hurt you or a family member or friend, isn't it? We know we need to forgive those who have wronged us, but it's not always easy. Sometimes it's downright difficult. But do you know what happens when we don't forgive? Our anger and hurt will begin to fester into an ugly sore in our minds and souls; the end result will be bitterness and a life void of joy.

At times we determine to do the right thing and forgive, only to have our efforts rejected. They don't want to accept our apology because they deny that they did anything wrong. When this happens, we must realize that the best thing we can do is to pray for God to heal the relationship and be open to His leading.

Sometimes our gesture of forgiveness may be interpreted as a way of manipulation, to try to get something from them, or to make them treat us better. Just remember that we cannot control anyone but ourselves. We should focus on our own attitudes and seek to genuinely forgive them in our hearts—whether they accept our forgiveness or not.

Thanks be to our Father that we don't ever have to worry about this kind of situation with Him. When we ask for His forgiveness, it's granted immediately. The slate is wiped clean and our relationship with Christ is fully restored. Oh, what joy floods our hearts when forgiven by the Savior.

Prayer: *Forgive me, Father, when I so often fail you. May I hide Your Word in my heart so passionately that I am sensitive to sin. When I do stumble or fall, prick my heart and draw me immediately to You for restoration. Help me to be kind, compassionate, and forgiving. Remind me that if I do not have a kind, compassionate, and forgiving heart, neither will I have Your joy.*

Have you had your Joy Juice today? Is your bitter becoming better with the Joy Juice of Jesus?

The past few days we've been looking at Ephesians 4. Some of the juice from these verses was hard to swallow. But the first two verses of Chapter Five give us some wise advice that will help us to make sure our Joy Juice is fragrant and sweet: ***"Be imitators of God, therefore, as dearly loved children and live a life of love, just as Christ loved us and gave himself up for us as a fragrant offering and sacrifice to God"*** **(Eph. 5:1, 2).**

Author Rick Renner explains: "Paul is telling us to model our lives after God. Just as a professional actor is committed to capturing the emotions, looks, voice, and character of the person he is portraying, we are to put our whole heart and soul into imitating God." [2]

Acting like God takes lots of practice. It's not going to come easily, and we will never attain perfection. But we can determine to start today and then try again tomorrow, the next day, and the next. Our goal should be to try to think like God, say the words He would say, and be confident in Him.

"Just as children imitate their parents, we should imitate God. His great love for us led him to sacrifice himself so that we might live. Our love for others should be a love that goes beyond affections to self-sacrificing service." [3]

When your heart is filled with this kind of love, all bitterness will cease. And it will be replaced with what is better—the joy of the Lord.

Prayer: *Sweet Father, how I want to be a fragment aroma in Your nostrils. May I so desire to be like You that I find myself imitating Jesus in every decision and every action I take. Allow me to have opportunities today in which I can be an example of Your love and joy.*

Have you had your Joy Juice today? Are you thinking sweet thoughts? It will certainly help you to have a more joyful day.

Many times we think that since our thoughts are private, they don't affect those around us. But this is far from true. Our thoughts not only touch others' lives, they also have a dramatic effect on our own. **Proverbs 23:7** says, *"For as he thinks in his heart, so is he"* (NKJV).

What kind of thoughts do you most often have? Are they kind or unkind? Are they peaceful or are they anxious? Are they bitter or better? You see, whatever we think most often, we become. If we think loving thoughts, we become loving. If we think anxious thoughts, we become anxious. If we think hateful thoughts. . .You see where we're going with this.

Next time we are tempted to focus on angry, bitter, resentful thoughts, let's ask God to wash those thoughts right out of our minds. None of us want to become an angry, bitter person. The enemy delights in filling our minds with wrong thoughts. With God's help, we can grasp hold of His strength, get those thoughts under control, and replace them with good, kind, loving thoughts.

So, as you go about your busy day, make sure to continually ask the Lord to help you to have a positive, peaceful, loving thought life. This is a major step toward bringing joy to others and having a joyful personal outlook on life.

Prayer: *Take control of my thought life, Father, and fill my mind with kind and loving thoughts. May I see people through Your eyes as You control my thought patterns, words, and reactions. Fill my mind with joyful thoughts.*

Have you had your Joy Juice today? It tastes a lot better if you are drinking it with a good attitude.

We all have days when our attitudes are not very joyful. Is it because of our thoughts? Think about it. When you notice your attitude going south, toward the negative, stop and examine the situation. I believe you'll find that the problem began with your thought life. In order to avoid thinking negatively, we must keep our thoughts renewed. **Ephesians 4:23** says, *"And be constantly renewed in the spirit of your mind"* (AMP).

How can we be sure that we are "constantly renewing" our thoughts and our attitudes? Think for a moment about the person who really gets on your last nerve. Do you find yourself thinking about all the reasons he irritates you? Do you replay in your mind over and over again the things she has said or done to hurt you?

1 Corinthians 2:16 reminds us that we have been given the *"mind of Christ."* But He will not force us to use it. We have to be intentional about thinking with the mind of Christ. When we accept Jesus as our Savior, we are a new creature; old things pass away and all things become new (2 Cor. 5:17)—even our thoughts.

May our continuous prayer be for God to renew our thoughts. Let's allow Him to take those negative thoughts and transform them into joyful ones.

Prayer: *Dear Father, I confess that many times my attitude is far from godly. Please take my negative, sometimes even bitter, thoughts and change them into the kind of thoughts with which you will be pleased. Renew my mind, continuously, Lord, beginning now. Give me a hunger and thirst for reading and studying Your Word, and help me to apply it to my daily life. Please draw me closer and closer to you so that my thoughts will be more like Yours. May I be a beacon of Your love and joy.*

Have you had your Joy Juice today? Notice how clear and transparent the juice is as you pour yourself a glass. Are your thoughts that transparent?

What if people could tell what you were thinking every minute? Would you be pleased with what they would learn about you? Though we know that God is all knowing and that He is intimately familiar with our thoughts, we don't always live like we believe that. Outwardly, we can pretend to be one kind of person, but on the inside, we may be something completely different. We may be able to mislead people, but there's no fooling God.

In **1 Chronicles 28:9** we read, *". . .the LORD searches every heart and understands every motive behind the thoughts."* What does He find when He searches your heart? Genuine love? Authenticity? Transparency? Or does He see a counterfeit, a phony? We can fool others, but God sees the real us when He looks at our heart.

Joyce Meyer challenges us:

If you have not been working with the Holy Spirit to break old thought patterns and form new ones, it is time to get started. Think some good thoughts about people, and as your atti-

tude starts to change toward them, watch your
relationships start to change for the better. [4]

Not only will your thoughts be more joyful, but
you will bring joy to others by allowing them to see
into your transparent heart.

Prayer: *As You search my heart, Lord, show me
where I need to change. I call on the Holy Spirit
today, now, right this moment, to take the blinders
off my heart and let me see the real me. Change my
heart and my thought patterns; replace them with the
attitude of Christ—one of love and joy.*

Have you had your Joy Juice today? As you sip your juice this morning, make sure your thoughts are joyful ones.

You know, we do have a choice about what kind of thoughts we entertain. Even in the midst of trials and troubles, we can still make a conscious choice to think good thoughts. Look at **Philippians 4:8**: *"Whatever is true, whatever is noble, whatever is right, whatever is pure, whatever is lovely, whatever is admirable—if anything is excellent or praiseworthy—think about such things."*

This verse would be an excellent life verse to hide in our hearts so that we can pull it out and use it as our weapon when negative circumstances arise and we're tempted to think bad thoughts. We are to think on things that are true, noble, and right—not untrue, despicable, and wrong. We are to focus on things that are pure, lovely, and admirable—not vulgar, ugly, and disrespectful. In this verse, Paul tells us to keep excellent and praiseworthy thoughts in our minds so that our daily lives will reflect His goodness and grace.

Frequently we are overwhelmed with situations that seem totally out of control. Instead of dwelling on the negatives and becoming discouraged, let's call to memory the verse in Philippians 4:8 and allow God to fill our minds with thoughts of joy.

Prayer: *May my thoughts be true, noble, right, pure, lovely, admirable, excellent, and praiseworthy. Help me to think on these kinds of things and stop focusing on any negatives. Overflow my mind with such joyful thoughts that they spill out onto those that cross my path today and every day.*

Have you had your Joy Juice today? Do you think your thinking is worth thinking about? I think it is.

Paul says in **2 Corinthians. 10:5** that we should *"take captive every thought to make it obedient to Christ."* He didn't say, "Don't think!" Nor did he say, "Take captive *some* of your thoughts." He said to take captive *every* thought.

In other words, when a thought pops into our minds, we must analyze it in a nanosecond. Is the thought beneficial to God's purpose or to my own? Is it destructive or selfish? Does it encourage and build up, or does it degrade and tear down?

Think about it this way: animals in a zoo are in captivity. Until they are released back into the wild, they will be in captivity. If the animals were kept in cages and were never fed, they would soon die. It is the same with our thoughts. If we feed a thought, it will keep growing—sometimes out of control. One seemingly harmless thought can become intensely destructive, not only to you, but also to your family, friends, and acquaintances. Your job may suffer. Your Christian testimony could be ruined. When your thoughts are uncontrolled, you can become an angry, bitter person with absolutely no joy in your life.

The next time a thought comes into your mind that is selfish, angry, jealous, or negative, pray and ask the Lord to help you "take the thought captive." Then, *"set your mind on things above, not on earthly things"* (Col. 3:2). Let's fix our thoughts on Jesus. He is willing to cleanse our lives and fill us with thoughts of joy.

Prayer: *Father, it is a challenge, to say the least, to keep my thoughts under control, to take them captive. So I ask You to help me. Redirect me, teach me, and control my thought patterns. Help me to see how destructive negative thoughts can be, making me bitter and resentful; let me see how they negatively affect those around me. Make my thoughts full of joy so that people will want this same joy of the Lord.*

Chapter Five

Tart and Tangy Harvest-Flavored Joy Juice

Have you had your Joy Juice today? It has a pumpkin flavor this time of year. Have you noticed?

During this season, we see pumpkins everywhere. They are used for decorations, desserts, snacks, and centerpieces. Families and school groups love to take a trip to the pumpkin patch and pick out their very own pumpkins.

One of my friends sent me an email a few days ago wishing me a "Happy Autumn." The words that accompanied the beautiful Fall picture made me look at pumpkins in a much different way. Here is what it said:

Being a Christian is like being a pumpkin. God lifts you up, takes you in, and washes all the dirt off of you. He opens you up, touches you deep inside, and scoops out all the yucky stuff—including the seeds of doubt, hate, greed, etc. Then He carves you a new smiling face and puts His light inside you to shine for all the world to see (Author unknown).

Isn't that a great analogy? Even though we don't all carve jack-o-lanterns, there is a truth here that is definitely for all of us. God is willing to take an ugly sinner and transform him into a delightful creation through which He can shine His light. The words in **Matthew 5:16** remind us that this is, indeed, God's plan for us: *". . .Let your light shine before men, that they may see your good deeds and praise your Father in heaven."*

Will you allow God to carve you into a shining example of His love and joy? Ask Him into your pumpkin patch today, and let Him begin His work in your heart and life.

Prayer: *Father, please take me and carve me according to Your perfect plan. Shine Your light brightly through me. Give me wisdom, understanding, and perseverance to withstand the carving process, for I realize that sometimes it's going to hurt. Remind me that it's all for my good and for Your glory. In the end, I will understand the delicious joy that comes from you.*

Have you had your Joy Juice today? It will help your faith to grow to unbelievable proportions.

I recently read an article telling of a young couple in Ohio who had a friendly rivalry going for several years to see who could grow the biggest pumpkin. In the Fall of 2009, it was the wife that brought home the honors. Her giant pumpkin set a new record, weighing in at 1,725 pounds. At one point, the massive pumpkin was growing thirty-three pounds a day. She kept it going by plying the soil with a mix of compost, coffee grounds, and cow manure. And, of course, she started with seeds of good genetics. [1]

As I thought about this prize winning pumpkin, I began to note how it parallels to our spiritual growth. If we want a winning relationship with Christ, we have to ply the soil of our heart and feed it the nutrients of Bible study and prayer. Sometimes God adds fertilizer, which is not sweet smelling, such as an unexpected trial in our lives. But He knows that in order for us to grow in our faith, we need the stuff that stinks along with the blessings that make us smile.

Just remember that the Master Gardener is always there. In **Matthew 13:31** Jesus reminds us that *"The kingdom of heaven is like a mustard seed..."* In some circumstances, we'll be able to feel our faith growing rapidly through the miracles that God is working out right before us. Other times, the growth process may be slow and painful. Throw out the bad seeds of anger, doubt, and bitterness, and plant your garden with the good seeds of love, peace, and hope. If you tend your garden using these nutrients, you are sure to grow a prize-winning joy.

Prayer: *Yes, Lord, I desire to be a prize-winning follower of Christ. Help me to **"press on toward the goal to win the prize for which God has called me heavenward in Christ Jesus"** (Phil. 3:14).*

Have you had your Joy Juice today? Isn't the pumpkin flavor delightful this time of year?

A pumpkin is, by definition, a round, orange winter squash. I never realized there were so many different varieties until I read of the farmer in California who boasts of planting eighty different kinds of pumpkins and squash. They range in size from miniature to jumbo. Some have a sweet taste and are best suited for pies and dessert recipes. Others are bland and have very little flavor, so they are used for other things, like decorating and carving. Even the colors vary from bright orange to pale yellow.

Our God is a God of variety. No two of us are alike. He takes the basic mold and continually comes up with new creations. We need to be content with whom He created us to be, but we must never be satisfied with what we can become in Him. He wants us continually to grow in our faith and develop a closer relationship with Him. There may be over a hundred different varieties of pumpkins and squash, but that number pales in comparison with how many ways we can serve our Master. He has created each of us with our own special abilities, strengths, and talents. Whatever variety you may be, God has a plan for you. When you are in the center of that plan, you'll find the indescribable joy that the scripture talks about in **1 Peter 1:8***: "Though you have not seen him, you love him; and even though you do not see him now, you believe in him and are filled with an inexpressible and glorious joy."*

Prayer: *Dear Lord, I am thankful for variety and that You have chosen me to be* me. *Help me to see my strengths and my weaknesses as Your perfect creation. Use me to accomplish Your will, and never let me become satisfied with my relationship with You. I desire to draw closer and closer and closer; You have promised that if I will draw close to You, then You will draw close to me. What joy that brings to my heart!*

Have you had your Joy Juice today? Pour yourself a large serving to go with that delicious slice of pumpkin pie.

I came across a website the other day suggesting activities to enjoy with children (<u>www.youthonline.ca</u>). In keeping with the fall theme, they were telling of fun things to make from and with pumpkins. They presented 101 different ideas. I never knew you do so many different things with a plain ole pumpkin. Listen to some of their suggestions:

- Pumpkin pie play dough
- Pumpkin raisin muffins
- Pumpkin soup
- Pumpkin rice krispies
- Snowman pumpkins
- Pumpkin pudding
- Pumpkin totem poles
- Pumpkin games, facts, art projects, recipes

The list goes on and on. Whoever came up with this many ideas not only liked pumpkins, but they obviously loved children.

But there is no comparison with all the countless expressions of God's love that He pours out on us continually. His list of blessings and ideas are endless.

1 Corinthians 2:9 tells us: *"No eye has seen, no ear has heard, no mind has conceived what God has prepared for those who love him."*

Let's not take for granted the love of our Father and the many ways He chooses to express that love to us, His children. Doesn't it fill your heart with joy to think of how much He loves you?

Prayer: *You have blessed me so much with your love, dear Father. I cannot even begin to list all the ways. When I begin to focus on the things that steal my joy, turn my heart and thoughts right back to you, the giver of all joy.*

Have you had your Joy Juice today? Would you like an extra serving with your pumpkin dessert? Have you ever thought about how many desserts can be made from pumpkins? It's not just pumpkin pie anymore. Just listen to some of the recipes I found:

- Spiced pumpkin doughnuts
- Double-decker pumpkin bread
- Autumn pear and pumpkin soup
- Pumpkin marmalade
- Pumpkin cream cheese spread
- Pumpkin praline cheese cake

Are you getting hungry yet? There are many, many recipes that can be found to make these delicious desserts, but they all have one thing in common: pumpkin. Some recipes call for fresh pumpkin, some for pumpkin out of a can. Others require the pumpkin to be chopped, while others say "mash" or "puree." Some snack recipes even use the seeds.

Just as there are many different recipes that can be cooked up from pumpkins, God has many different ways to use us so that we can serve Him. We all are His creations, but He used many different recipes. We should be thankful for how He made us and sing

His praises as the psalmist did in **Psalm 139:14:** *"I praise you because I am fearfully and wonderfully made".*

Some people have a flavor very different from your flavor, but it takes all kinds and varieties to spice up life and accomplish His purpose. The important thing is to be willing to be used of Him. When you are in His kitchen, giving him full, complete control of the recipe, He is sure to bake up a delicious end product. And it always goes well with Joy Juice.

Prayer: *Dear Lord Jesus, show me the recipe that you have planned for me. Give me wisdom enough to follow Your instructions so that a delicious product of joy will be served up to all those within my sphere of influence.*

A SPECIAL RECIPE OF JOY JUICE FOR THANKSGVING WEEK

Have you had your Joy Juice today? The batch of Joy Juice for the next few days is a special recipe intended for you as part of your Thanksgiving celebration. Let's make sure we are drinking it faithfully so that we'll find our hearts to be thankful.

Ever heard the question, "Which came first: the chicken or the egg?" Well, here's another one for you to ponder: "Are we thankful because we're joyful, or are we joyful because we're thankful?"

Genuine joy comes from having a thankful heart. That means being appreciative for the things that we have, instead of concentrating on what we don't have. It means being satisfied and content with what God has blessed us with instead of being jealous of what someone else has. There will always be those who have more materially than you and me. But is that really what's important? Let's take a lesson from Paul.

He begins his letter to the Philippians with thanks. Though he wrote this letter from a prison cell, he included joyful words: *"I thank my God every time*

I remember you. In all my prayers for all of you I always pray with joy" (**Phil. 1:3, 4**).

Could you pray with joy if you were in a prison cell? Paul could because he realized that he had what was important: a relationship with Christ. Is Jesus your top priority? Is He so important that you can look beyond your circumstances and remain thankful, regardless?

Like Paul, let's thank God and pray with joy.

Prayer: *Dear Heavenly Father, on this Thanksgiving week, may I stop long enough to realize how blessed I am. Remind me that I have so many reasons to be joyful. Regardless of what's going in my life, if I had nothing else, I always have you. That is reason enough to be filled with thanksgiving and joy.*

Have you had your Joy Juice today? This week of Thanksgiving is a wonderful time to keep plenty of Joy Juice within easy reach.

We all have so much for which to be thankful, don't we? If each of us would write down our blessings, the list would be endless. Begin right now mentally noting some of those things for which you feel blessed and grateful. It might be family, friends, a home, your job, good health, a wonderful church family, and of course, I would add grandchildren. The list could go on and on.

Indeed, we are blessed, but do we always express our thankfulness? So often we take our blessings for granted. **Psalm 100** is a psalm of thanksgiving. The Psalmist tells us to *"Shout for joy to the LORD."* Most of the time, we don't even whisper our gratitude, do we? We certainly don't shout. If we would begin to make a conscious effort to focus on the goodness of God in our lives—how He is with us through the tough times, as well as the good and how He is our provider and protector—we might find ourselves so filled with joy that we would truly feel like shouting.

This Thanksgiving, let's be intentional about expressing our thanks to our Father in Heaven Who is the giver of all things. Thank Him for His goodness and faithfulness. A grateful heart is a joyful heart. So, give the Lord a joyful shout.

Prayer: *"Come, let us sing for joy to the LORD; let us shout aloud to the Rock of our salvation. Let us come before him with thanksgiving and extol him with music and song"* **(Psalm 95:1, 2).** May this be my prayer throughout this Thanksgiving week, Father. Remind me that every day should be a celebration of thanks and joy.

Have you had your Joy Juice today? Today is Thanksgiving "Eve." The day before turkey day is time to take care of all those last minute details to make sure you're ready for the big day. Make sure to stock up on Joy Juice.

Many of us are looking forward to family coming in for the holidays. We'll be consumed with grocery shopping, cooking, straightening our house, and getting the yards clean so that we can be ready for our guests. But are we missing the point? Don't you think that we should slow down a little and take time to count our blessings during this season? There is an old hymn that I can remember singing that tells us to "Count your many blessings, name them one by one...and it will surprise you what the Lord hath done." [2]

When we stay too busy to recognize all that God has done and is doing in our lives, then we are too busy. May I suggest that you take a few minutes to meditate on the goodness of God as you go about your day? Go to the book of Psalms and read some of the beautiful verses that were penned by men who loved God. They will remind you to be thankful. **Psalm 28:7** says, *"My heart leaps for joy and I will give thanks to him in song."*

I know you've got a busy day planned. So go ahead, and start hopping. But first allow your heart to "leap for joy" in thankful praise to God.

Prayer: *Father, there is much to do today to get ready for the big day tomorrow. Please help me to slow down and count my blessings. When I concentrate on all you have done for me, indeed, my heart leaps for joy. I love You, and I thank You for pouring out Your blessings of joy into my heart and life.*

THANKSGIVING DAY DELIGHT

Have you had your Joy Juice today? Happy Thanksgiving! Are you serving lots of Joy Juice at your Thanksgiving Feast?

For a day that is unforgettable, greet your guests, whether family or friends, with a heart of gratitude. Though many of us will be busy cooking, serving, and entertaining, we can still demonstrate an attitude of gratitude. Instead of getting stressed about all we have to do (like poor Martha did in Luke 10), let's take a cue from her sister, Mary, and concentrate on what is most important—sitting at the feet of Jesus. He said that Mary had chosen what was better.

Why not stop right now and choose what is better? Meditate on **Psalm 100:**

Shout for joy to the LORD, all the earth.
   Worship the Lord with gladness;
   come before him with joyful songs.
Know that the Lord is God.
   It is he who made us, and we are
      his;
   we are his people, the sheep of his
      pasture.

Enter his gates with thanksgiving
and his courts with praise;
give thanks to him and praise his
name.
For the Lord is good and his love
endures forever;
his faithfulness continues through
all generations.

Now, don't you feel better starting the day with God's Word? It's up to you to whisper your personal prayer of thanksgiving. Make sure it overflows with joy.

Prayer: *God, you are my Provider, and I thank You for the abundance of Your provision. Help me not to take for granted my blessings, but make me aware of all that I can enjoy simply because of Your love for me. On this Thanksgiving Day, may my heart overflow with gratitude for all my blessings, large and small. Most of all, Father, I praise You for sending Your Son Jesus to die for me. The security of my salvation through You makes me feel like "shouting for joy."*

Have you had your Joy Juice today? After eating that big Thanksgiving meal yesterday, you might need an antacid with your Joy Juice.

Most of us probably did eat too much turkey and dressing and all the trimmings. But aren't we thankful that we live in a country where food is usually plentiful? Many people throughout this world are hungry. We are a blessed nation. Even though we are in a time of uncertainty, we still have lots for which to be thankful.

We've just celebrated THANKSgiving Day. But should we wait for the fourth Thursday in November every year to express our thanks? Of course not! It should be a constant condition of the heart. **1 Thessalonians 5:16-18** instructs us to *"Be joyful always; pray continually; give thanks in all circumstances, for this is God's will for you in Christ Jesus."*

Do you notice how being joyful and praying go hand in hand with giving thanks? That's the key. Every day we should go to God in prayer and thank Him for all the blessings that are ours. Name them specifically. You'll notice a sweet, joyful spirit bubbling in your heart, a heart filled with gratitude. Celebrate Thanksgiving every day, and you will find yourself focusing on the things that truly bring you joy.

Prayer: *Father, remind me that every day should be a day of Thanksgiving. I desire to experience and express Your joy each day, but I know that in order to do so, I must have a heart of thanksgiving. May I never take lightly the gifts that You so richly pour out into my life.*

Chapter Six

Warm Spiced
Joy Juice Cider
For the
Christmas Holidays

჻

(This batch of Joy Juice was cooked up for sipping throughout the month of December—in preparation for Christmas.)

Have you had your Joy Juice today? With the hustle and bustle of the holidays, we'd better drink lots of Joy Juice to keep us in the spirit of the season.

Countless people miss the real meaning of Christmas completely. Stores started weeks ago pulling out their Christmas decorations and stocking their shelves for early shoppers. Many of us have begun making our lists and agonizing over what to get our family members this year. Our calendars are filling up quickly with numerous Christmas parties and dinners, as well as family gatherings and times of gift swapping. Oh, and let's not forget, we've got to decorate our house, make Christmas candy for the neighbors, practice for the church Christmas program, and attend the school Christmas sing-a-long.

Whew! I'm tired already, and it's just the first of December. Let's take a big swig of Joy Juice and think about this for a minute. What is this season all about? To see how much busyness we can pack into the month? OR is it about experiencing the joy of Jesus? Just consider that we would have no reason to celebrate if it were not for the birth of Christ.

Why don't we make a conscious effort to truly enjoy Christmas this year and remember what the angel said in **Luke 2:10**: *"I bring you good news of great joy that will be for all the people."*

Prayer: *The angel brought "good tidings of great joy." Father, help me to remember that good news throughout this Christmas season. Help me not to get so busy doing good things that I forget what is best—the birth of Your Son, Jesus. Oh, what joy!*

Have you had your Joy Juice today? I believe that children drink gobs of Joy Juice during this season of the year.

Observe the little children that you see today. The wonder in their sparkling eyes, the excitement in their voices, the squeals of delight when they see the lights and packages all serve to express their excitement over Christmas. I can remember as a little girl being so thrilled when the Wishbook catalog came in the mail. I would ponder and drool over the pages in that book, wishing for many of the items to be under my tree on Christmas morning. That book was falling apart by the time Christmas arrived.

Even though my parents were careful to keep things in perspective, I'm afraid my focus was in the wrong place. I knew we were celebrating Jesus' birthday, but I don't think I really understood the significance of his birth. As adults, we have to be careful not to get caught up in the hurry and worry of the holidays. We should teach our children about the real reason for the season.

This year, let's put our focus on the best gift of all: *"Thanks be to God for his indescribable gift!"* **(2 Cor. 9:15).** God has already sent His love to us wrapped in the form of his Son, Jesus. When we open that glorious gift, our focus will not be on material things. Instead, we will desire what's in the best book of all, the Bible, God's Word. That promises to bring a joyful Christmas to all of us.

Prayer: *Thank you, Father, for the comforting truth that we do not need to have a wish book or wish list. We can bring our needs and desires to You any time, anywhere. Thank You for always hearing our requests and giving us what is best. As Christmas draws closer, make me extra joyful due to the "indescribable gift" that You have given me—joy in Jesus.*

Have you had your Joy Juice today? During this Christmas season, please don't forget to add Joy Juice to your shopping list.

How do we share joy with others? Let's remember that joy and happiness are two different things. Happiness depends on our circumstances, what's happening in our lives. Joy, however, depends on Jesus. We can do as **Philippians 4:4** reminds us and *"Rejoice in the Lord always"* if we'll keep Jesus as our focus this Christmas. Sure, we have many fun activities like parades and parties and shopping and baking. But if we take our eyes off the *real reason* that we are celebrating, then we will lose our joy.

So what can we do to assure that we are keeping our focus on Christ this CHRISTmas? Here are a few suggestions:

- Start your day with a prayer of gratitude, thanking God for the birth of His Son, Jesus.
- Read the Christmas story from your Bible. Why not let that be your daily devotionals during this entire month? You can find the story of Jesus' birth in the Gospels of Matthew, Mark, Luke, and John.

- When you decorate your home, try to find a nativity that will be a visual reminder of the birth of Jesus.
- Worship faithfully in the church of your choice. To gather with fellow Christians during any time of year is special, but at Christmas it's extra joyful.

These suggestions are just for starters. Try to think of other ways to invite Christ into your Christmas this year.

Prayer: *Jesus, You are the reason we are celebrating Christmas. Help me not to leave You out of my heart and home. May the Holy Spirit prick my heart and make me super sensitive to be intentional about keeping You first—during the Christmas season, as well as every other day during the year. "Joy to the world, the Lord has come!"*

Have you had your Joy Juice today? Are you taking the time to sip some hot spiced Joy Juice cider as you focus on the real reason for the season?

Luke 2: 6 & 7 tells us that while Joseph and Mary were in Bethlehem, *"the time came for the baby to be born, and she gave birth to her firstborn, a son. She wrapped him in cloths and placed him in a manger, because there was no room for them in the inn."*

Though I know that all of this was God's perfect plan, I've always felt a little sadness that there was "no room for them in the inn." Just think about how uncomfortable that stable must have been for Mary. She had to give birth (painful), not in a nice hospital room and not even in the comfort of her own home. She gave birth to the King of Kings in a smelly, damp, dirty stable. His bed was a manger filled with hay *"because there was no room for them in the inn."*

This Christmas let's ask ourselves if we have made room in our hearts for Him. We would have no reason to celebrate Christmas if it were not for the birth of our Savior. If we will make Christ a priority, this Christmas will be filled with a special kind of indescribable joy.

Prayer: *Dear Jesus, there is room in my heart for You. Please come in and take residence in my heart and life. Make this Christmas season extra special because of the joy that comes from having You as my personal Savior and Lord.*

Have you had your Joy Juice today? Well, we've started off the month of December sipping on the warm, sweet Joy Juice of Jesus' birth. I'm excited about how this Christmas is going to be extra special for those of you who are committed to the intentional decision to keep Christ in Christmas.

When Jesus is our priority, it becomes much easier to see His hand in all things.

Even when we are going through tough times, whether financial or physical, emotionally or spiritual, we can have joy because our faith is in Him. For some people the holidays are a sad time because they have lost loved ones. Others have been through a divorce or are separated from beloved family members due to circumstances beyond their control. Some people dread the holidays for a variety of reasons.

Whatever emotions you are experiencing about this time of year, always remember that God loves you. He loves you so much that He sent His Son just for you. And as we approach this Christmas season, we can depend on that love to continue to be there for us. **Psalm 55:22** tells us to *"Cast your burden upon the LORD and He will sustain you"* (NASB).

Never hesitate to give Him your concerns. Lay them at His feet so that you can experience strength in Him. That's the kind of joy that He wants you to have as your special Christmas gift this year. Won't you accept His valuable gift?

Prayer: *Father, I can hide nothing from You. You know my feelings about this time of year. If my emotions and thoughts are anything but joyful, convict my heart and remind me that because of Jesus' birth, I can have peace and comfort. When I begin to be overwhelmed with all the busyness of the season, remind me to be still and "cast my burdens on You." Thank you! I already feel much more joyful.*

Have you had your Joy Juice today? May I suggest that you give some as Christmas gifts this year?

So often we get caught up in the "what I want for Christmas" mode. We begin to drop hints to our family and friends about what we really need. In most families, Christmas lists are made and shared weeks before Christmas ever gets here. We spend a lot of time thinking about what we want to get for Christmas.

We already have the best gift of all—God's son, Jesus. What a gift of love! God sacrificed His son, so that we might know the joy of the Lord as our strength. Let's think about how we can pass that love and joy on to others during this Christmas season.

One way that we can share Christ's love is simply to follow the instruction of **Philippians 2:3-4**: *"Do nothing out of selfish ambition or vain conceit, but in humility consider others better than yourselves. Each of you should look not only to your own interests, but also to the interests of others."* Paul was encouraging us to take our eyes off of ourselves, our wants, our desires, and our rights and to think of others instead.

So this Christmas season, let's stop thinking so much of our own agenda and begin to look around to see how we can help someone else. You'll be surprised at how much joy will be in your heart when you share the joy of Jesus with others.

Prayer: *During this Christmas season, it is my desire, Lord, to experience a grateful heart. Instead of pondering what I want for Christmas, help me to remember that I already have the most wonderful gift of all. Help me to take my eyes off of self and focus on you and how I can serve You. Give me unexpected opportunities to share Your love and joy with others.*

Have you had your Joy Juice today? For a unique Christmas gift idea, why not give a case of Joy Juice to every person on your gift list?

Yesterday we talked about getting our eyes off ourselves and putting aside our wants and selfish desires. We decided that this Christmas we are going to be intentional about sharing the love and joy of the Lord with others, right? I thought that's what you said.

I have another great Christmas gift idea that is very economical and certainly demonstrates the love and joy of Jesus. I love this gift myself. And I promise you everyone on your list—no matter what age, no matter their gender, regardless of their interests or talents—will be thrilled with this gift. It's the gift of encouragement.

Author Karen Porter says that "encouragement is like a chocolate candy kiss. Even a small piece yields a wonderful result, and we find ourselves looking forward eagerly to the next taste. In the same way, just a word of encouragement hints at the love of a friend and leaves us wanting more." [1] We are instructed in **1 Thessalonians 5:11** to *"encourage one another and build each other up."*

Ask God to make you sensitive to others during this Christmas season. You may never know what a difference this simple gift will make in the life of that person who is in need of God's joy.

Prayer: *Dear Lord, bring people into my path that need that encouraging word or kind gesture. Give me wisdom to know exactly what they need to be lifted up. Speak through me and use me as a vessel to draw them closer to You. May they see Jesus in me; that would be the best Christmas gift I could give them. What joy would fill my heart to be used by You in this way.*

Have you had your Joy Juice today? It's a great energy booster. Have you been running and racing, trying to get everything done before the big day arrives? Don't forget how important Joy Juice is to your spiritual stamina during this busy Christmas season.

Life is a race. And sometimes we get tired and discouraged, especially during the busy holidays. Long distance runners tell me that as they near the end of a long race, their legs ache, their throat burns, and their whole body cries out to quit. But then they hear the people at the finish line cheering them on. And that bit of encouragement helps the runner to push through the pain all the way to the end.

The same is true with us in the race of life. **1 Thessalonians 5:11** tells us to "***build each other up***." Point out to someone a quality that you appreciate in him or her. Tell a co-worker what a good job they did on a project. Express your appreciation for someone's talent or ability. And please don't forget that our family members need to hear words of edification as well. As a matter of fact, don't you agree that most of us would prefer a steady gifting of encouragement to a material gift that's going to tear up or soon go out of style?

Put encouragement at the top of your gift list this Christmas. It will bring joy to the person as they open it and joy to you as you see the smile light up their face.

Prayer: *As I race about, trying to get all my Christmas shopping and projects completed, Lord, don't let me forget that the best gifts are the ones that can't be bought. Show me specific people today that really need a gift of encouragement. Then use me to be Your mouthpiece or instrument of joy.*

Have you had your Joy Juice today? Still trying to decide what to give some of your friends or family members for Christmas? You can always give a generous portion of Joy Juice.

Many of us are being cautious about what we spend because of the state of our economy and because we are trying to be good stewards of what God has given us financially. We've discovered there are many valuable gifts that we can give that will cost us nothing but our time, effort, and love. Indeed, it is important that we put others before ourselves, helping those in need and gifting them with encouragement.

Are you looking for a unique gift idea for your boss for Christmas or for someone who is a leader in your church or community? The passage in 1 **Thessalonians 5:12 & 13** gives some good gift suggestions: *"Now, we ask you, brothers, to respect those who work hard among you, who are over you in the Lord and who admonish you. Hold them in the highest regard in love because of their work."*

The gifts of respect and honor are encouraged in these verses. How do we show respect? How do we "hold others in highest regard"? We can express our appreciation, telling them how we have been helped by their leadership. We can thank them for their ministry and influence in our life. If we say nothing, how will they ever know? Remember, even those is high offices of leadership need our love and support. And what a great way to let the joy of Jesus shine during this blessed Christmas season.

Prayer: *Heavenly Father, touch my heart and bring to mind at least one leader that You want me to encourage this Christmas season. Allow me to share in a genuine and joyful way the respect and honor that he/she deserves.*

Have you had your Joy Juice today? Do you have your Christmas shopping done? Or have you even started? You can always give the gift of joy. It doesn't cost a penny, but, oh, how it lasts.

I know that we all enjoy new things and at Christmas time we express our love for others by giving gifts. But let's not get so caught up in the gifts that we miss what is truly important. We've been discussing how we should strive to keep Jesus the focus of our Christmas. We've talked about the gifts of putting others first, encouraging our friends and family members, and giving respect and honor. May I suggest one more gift idea? This one *will* cost you. It's called T- I-M-E.

First, we should spend time alone with God. Read His Word and seek His guidance through the Scripture. We should spend time in prayer, thanking Him for His *"indescribable gift"* of Jesus (**2 Cor. 9:15**). When our hearts are in tune with Him because of the time we have spent in His presence, then we will be able to see more clearly what is truly important. Parents, spending time with your children is a precious gift. They would rather have you and your attention than any present that can be bought. Remember, *"There is* *a time for everything, and a season for every activity under heaven."* **(Ecclesiastes 3:1).**

This Christmas set aside time to spend with your special someone. You don't have to spend a dime—just some quality time. This may be their favorite Christmas gift of all—a gift wrapped in joy.

Prayer: *Sweet Jesus, thank you for always being willing and available to spend time with me. May I follow Your example and make the time to spend with those I love. If there is someone that really needs special time and attention during this Christmas season, please open my eyes to their need. Use me to spread Your Christmas joy.*

Have you had your Joy Juice today? Most of us are busy getting ready for Christmas. If we're not drinking our Joy Juice, we might forget what the season is all about.

Many people began readying their homes for Christmas as soon as Thanksgiving was over—or before. Today let's think about some of the symbols of Christmas that we use to decorate during this season. Why do we use certain items to bring that holiday cheer into our homes?

Consider the wreath that traditionally hangs on our front door each Christmas. The circle of the wreath reminds us of God's eternal, everlasting love for us. It has no beginning or end. **Psalm 136:26** reminds us to *"Give thanks to the God of heaven. His love endures forever."* The greenery used in most wreaths is to represent the truth that Christ lives and came to earth to give us the opportunity for eternal life. The familiar passage in **John 3:16** is such a sweet reminder of why we are to celebrate: *"For God so loved the world that he gave his one and only Son, that whoever* (that's you and me) *believes in him shall not perish but have eternal life."*

I don't know about you, but my Christmas wreath has already taken on a whole new look, a look that will shine with the joy of the Lord throughout our Christmas holidays.

Prayer: *Each time I see a wreath this Christmas season, Father, may I be reminded of Your never-ending love. It has no beginning and no end. Hallelujah! What a reason to be joyful.*

Have you had your Joy Juice today? You may find some under your Christmas tree this year.

Many of us have begun decorating for the Christmas holidays. Yesterday we hung our wreath on the front door and were reminded of God's eternal love. Today let's get our tree ready for the holidays.

One story that I researched said that Martin Luther is responsible for the origin of the Christmas tree. This story says that "one Christmas Eve, about the year 1500, he was walking through the snow-covered woods and was struck by the beauty of the snow glistened trees. Their branches, dusted with snow, shimmered in the moon light. When he got home, he set up a small fir tree and shared the story with his children. He decorated the Christmas tree with small candles, which he lighted in honor of Christ's birth." [2]

Some people may not believe in putting up a tree for Christmas. And that's perfectly okay. But we can all believe that many years ago, God sent his son to earth in the form of a baby boy. This happened as the prophet Isaiah had foretold:

"Therefore the Lord himself will give you a sign: The virgin will be with child and will give birth to a son, and will call him Immanuel" **(Isaiah 7:14).**

Because of Jesus, we can celebrate Christmas with exceeding, abundant joy in our hearts.

Prayer: *As we trim the tree or simply meditate on Jesus' birth, may we be reminded of Your faithfulness, Lord. Thank You for speaking through Your prophet Isaiah, so that we have record of this miraculous prophecy as it unfolded. As we enjoy the beautiful Christmas lights this year, let them serve as a reminder that you are the light of the world. You are the real Christmas gift of hope and joy.*

Have you had your Joy Juice today? As you decorate your home for Christmas, why don't you consider serving Joy Juice to all those who help with this task? It'll make the time pass quickly and joyfully.

Speaking of decorating, everywhere we look this month we see beautiful expressions of the season—one of which is the lovely poinsettia. This flower was first called "The Flower of the Holy Night." A Mexican legend tells of a poor child who had nothing to give the baby Jesus. He picked some weeds to give as a gift to the Christ-child. When he brought his gift to the manger, the weeds were miraculously transformed into beautiful star-like flowers. [3] (The flower is named for a man named Poinsett, the American ambassador to Mexico, who is given credit for introducing it to the United States.)

Though this is just a legend, we know the truth is found in Jesus' birth. Often believers refer to Jesus as the "Lily of the Valley." A lily is a sweet and fragrant flower. **Ephesians 5:2** describes Jesus as the One Who *"loved us and gave himself up for us as a fragrant offering and sacrifice to God."* The King James Version uses the terminology *"sweet-smelling savor."* If Christ willingly gave His life for us, then we should certainly put Him first on our Christmas list. Decorate your heart with the "Lily of the Valley." Your life will shine with the joy of Jesus, the reason for the season.

Prayer: *Precious Lily of the Valley, indeed, You are a "fragrant offering." As we celebrate this blessed Christmas season, may I keep You first in all that I do. Each time I see a Poinsettia, touch my heart to send up a prayer of gratitude for Your supreme sacrifice. Thank you, Jesus, that Your story is not a legend, but truth—overflowing with joy.*

Have you had your Joy Juice today? It's the perfect drink to quench your thirst as you go about getting ready for Christmas. How 'bout a candy cane to snack on with your juice this morning?

The story is told that many years ago, a candy maker wanted to make a Christmas candy that would serve as a witness to his Christian faith. He began with a stick of pure white, hard candy—white to symbolize the virgin birth and the sinless nature of Jesus, and hard—to symbolize the solid rock, the foundation of the Church.

The candy maker made the candy in the form of a "J" to represent the name of

Jesus, our Savior. He thought it could also represent the staff of the Good Shepherd. Throughout the Bible, Jesus is referred to as our Shepherd. In **John 10:11** Jesus Himself said, *"I am the good shepherd. The good shepherd lays down his life for the sheep."* In **verse 14** He goes on to say, *"I am the good shepherd; I know my sheep and my sheep know me."* The red stripes on the candy cane were to represent the blood shed by Christ on the cross so that we could have the promise of eternal life. [4]

This year, as you snack on the traditional candy cane as a treat or use it as a decoration, remember the origin of the candy cane and celebrate the joy of Jesus.

Prayer: *Good Shepherd, I praise You for leading me, protecting me, feeding me, and loving me. May the traditional candy cane become anything but traditional as I see it through a different set of eyes. Come, Lord Jesus, and live in my heart this Christmas season and in all the days to come. As I taste the sweetness of Jesus, please fill my heart with joy.*

Have you had your Joy Juice today? It's sure to bring you lots of Christmas cheer.

We've talked this week about some of the traditions of Christmas. We've hung the wreath in honor of God's unending love; we've put up our Christmas tree and decorated our surroundings with beautiful poinsettias. We've even used candy canes as a reminder of Jesus, our Shepherd. I think we may be ready to place those gifts under the tree.

Why do we give gifts at Christmas time? Do we do it out of obligation? Are we just trying to keep score because someone has given us a gift? If we give with this attitude, then gift-giving will be a chore rather than a joy. Let's take a lesson from the Magi who came to see the baby Jesus.

Look at **Matthew 2:10, 11**: *"When they saw the star, they were overjoyed. On coming to the house, they saw the child with his mother Mary, and they bowed down and worshipped him. Then they opened their treasures and presented him with gifts of gold and of incense and of myrrh."* Their act of giving was an expression of love and honor.

This Christmas as we give our Christmas gifts to loved ones, let us first stop to worship our Savior, as did the Magi. If we will put Him first, then our giving to others will be a reflection of the joy of Jesus.

Prayer: *Dear Jesus, first and foremost I acknowledge that You are the greatest gift of all. During this Christmas season, help me not to get so caught up in the gift buying and giving/receiving that I forget why we are celebrating. I desire for this Christmas to have special meaning. I give myself to You as my sacrificial gift back to You. Use me to spread Your joy to those You bring into my path this Christmas season.*

seventy mile trip to pay his taxes. Mary, who had to go with him, was expecting her baby any time. And they couldn't find anywhere to stay except a stable.

These two were in the perfect will of God, yet they were in uncomfortable circumstances. You see, when we do God's will, we're not guaranteed a life of comfort and ease. We *are* promised that all things—even our discomfort—have meaning in God's plan. What a Christmas gift of love, hope, and joy!

Prayer: *Thank you, God, for sending your Son, Jesus. I know that it was within Your power to let Him be born in a palace suitable for a King, but You chose to let Him be born in a stable. When I begin to complain about the uncomfortable times in my life, please remind me of what Jesus did for me. Oh, what joy should flood my heart!*

Have you had your Joy Juice today? Why don't you curl up with a warm cupful as we read more of the Christmas story today?

Yesterday we read from **Luke 2** and were reminded of why Joseph and Mary went to the little town of Bethlehem. Let's read **verses 6 & 7**: *"While they were there, the time came for the baby to be born, and she gave birth to her firstborn, a son. She wrapped him in cloths and placed him in a manger, because there was no room for them in the inn."*

Like a good mother, Mary was prepared in case the baby was born while they were on their trip to pay their taxes. She had packed swaddling cloths to keep the baby warm and to wrap him snuggly to give him the sense of security that new babies like. She wrapped him in cloths and placed him in a manger— a feeding trough for animals. No matter how clean the stable was kept, the fact is that the surroundings at Jesus' birth were dark and dirty. It was certainly not the kind of place the Jews expected as the birth-place of the Messiah King.

How often do we limit God by our own expecta-tions? Keep in mind that He is at work even when we don't see Him—even in the dirty, dark stables of our lives.

CHRISTMAS EVE SERVING

Have you had your Joy Juice today? Perk a big pot full because it's Christmas Eve.

As a child, I would get excited beyond description every Christmas Eve. My siblings and I could hardly go to sleep because of the joyful anticipation of what Christmas morning would bring. Now, as an adult, I realize what I should have been more excited about…the birthday of the King.

Let's go back to our Christmas story in *Luke 2:8-11* and read about the excitement of another group, the shepherds:

And there were shepherds living out in the fields nearby, keeping watch over their flocks at night. An angel of the Lord appeared to them, and the glory of the Lord shone around them, and they were terrified. But the angel said to them, "Do not be afraid. I bring you good news of great joy that will be for all the people. Today in the town of David a Savior has been born to you; he is Christ the Lord."

Talk about a birth announcement. At first the shepherds were afraid, but their fear was transformed into great joy when they heard the good news. Their Savior had been born—our Savior.

On this Christmas Eve, let's ask God to fill our hearts with the wonder of this blessed event, the birth of our Savior Jesus Christ. Ask Him for that child-like excitement and anticipation. Excitement not for the gifts we'll receive tonight or tomorrow but for the gift we have already received. Accept Him with great joy.

Prayer: *Blessed Savior, I never want to lose the excitement of celebrating You. On this eve of Christmas, may I not get so caught up in the busyness that I forget why I need to be genuinely excited. As the angels sang, "Glory to God in the highest!" (Luke 2:14)*

WARM, SPICED JOY JUICE TO BE SERVED ON CHRISTMAS DAY

Have you had your Joy Juice today? It's Christmas Day, the perfect time for celebrating and sharing the joy of the Lord.

As the old carol so beautifully exclaims, "Joy to the World, the Lord is come! Let earth receive her King!" Isaac Watts wrote the lyrics to this song three hundred years ago in 1710. And still today the words can be heard throughout the world, heralding Christ's birth. Sing the words—at least in your heart:

Joy to the World, the Lord is come!
Let earth receive her King;
Let every heart prepare Him room,
And Heaven and nature sing,
And Heaven and nature sing,
And Heaven, and Heaven, and nature sing.

Joy to the World, the Savior reigns!
Let men their songs employ;
While fields and floods, rocks, hills and plains
Repeat the sounding joy,

Repeat the sounding joy,
Repeat, repeat, the sounding joy.

No more let sins and sorrows grow,
Nor thorns infest the ground;
He comes to make His blessings flow
Far as the curse is found,
Far as the curse is found,
Far as, far as, the curse is found.

He rules the world with truth and grace,
And makes the nations prove
The glories of His righteousness,
And wonders of His love,
And wonders of His love,
And wonders, wonders, of His love.

This is the day we have set aside to honor the birth of Jesus. Let's not lose that truth amidst all the packages and people and food and fun. Sure, it's a wonderful blessing to be able to share this day with our loved ones. But steal away for a private moment and whisper a prayer of thanks to God for His *"indescribable gift"* of Jesus. **(2 Cor. 9:15)**

Let's celebrate His birth throughout this Christmas day. If you have children, lead them in a verse of "Happy Birthday, Dear Jesus." Singing is a wonderful way to praise and worship our Savior. The angels sang in *Luke 2:13, 14: "And suddenly there was with the angel a multitude of the heavenly host praising God and saying, 'Glory to God in the highest, and on earth peace, good will toward men!'"* (KJV).

Prayer: *Sing a song of praise and prayer to the Lord today.*

Have you had your Joy Juice today? Hope you had plenty to last through Christmas.

How quickly Christmas Day came and went. Hopefully, we'll find ourselves slowing down from the busy holiday rush. But will we forget why we've been celebrating? Let's take the joy of Christmas and share it with those we see each day.

That's what the shepherds did in *Luke 2:15-20:*

When the angels had left them and gone into heaven, the shepherds said to one another, 'Let's go to Bethlehem and see this thing that has happened, which the Lord has told us about.' So they hurried off and found Mary and Joseph, and the baby, who was lying in the manger. When they had seen him, they spread the word concerning what had been told them about his child, and all who heard it were amazed at what the shepherds said to them. But Mary treasured up all these things and pondered them in her heart. The shepherds returned, glorifying and praising God for all the things they had heard and seen, which were just as they had been told.

These shepherds were overjoyed at the revelation of the truth, and they went about excitedly spreading the word. How about you and me? Do our lives reflect that kind of excitement? Though Christmas Day is over, let's strive to joyfully and excitedly take the good news with us wherever we go, no matter what day it is. What better way is there to share the joy of the Lord?

Prayer: *May every day be like Christmas Day, dear Jesus, as I meditate on the wonder of Your birth. Help me to be like the shepherds who could not wait to tell what they had witnessed. I, too, have seen You. You are everywhere: in the miracle of birth, in the beauty of creation, in the warm embrace of those I love. Remind me to glorify and praise you in all things, large and small. Thank You for that special batch of Christmas Joy Juice that You have served me this season.*

Chapter Seven

Joy Juice "Lite"

Springtime Servings

Have you had your Joy Juice today? You might need a fresh batch since the seasons have changed, and it's now springtime.

Don't you love the change of seasons? I don't understand all the complex, scientific explanations for the changes. Some people say it's the angle at which the sunlight touches the earth's surface, the tilt of the earth's axis, and the position of the sun in the sky. What I do understand is that no matter what all the intricate details may be, we can sum it up in one word: God,

In **Genesis 1:14** we read, *"And God said, 'Let there be lights in the expanse of the sky to separate the day from the night, and let them serve as signs to mark seasons and days and years'. "*

Our Creator knew we needed the change of the seasons. He likes variety and knows that we do, too. After a long, hot summer, isn't autumn refreshing? Then come the winter months when we bundle up for the cold days and nights. By the time we get really tired of the cold, then comes the spring with warmer weather, sunshine, and gorgeous flowers budding and blooming.

If we will stop and reflect on the goodness of our Creator, we will not only be basking in springtime beauty, but we will also be seeing a new joy with each flower that blooms. Listen carefully, and you may even hear the birds singing their new song called "Springtime Joy."

Prayer: *"I've got the joy, joy, joy, joy down in my heart!" Thank you, Father, for the gift of the seasons. Help me to always see You in the beauty of nature and the changing of the seasons. There is joy all around me; don't let me miss it.*

Have you had your Joy Juice today? As you enjoy your juice this morning, gaze out your window and notice the beautiful signs of spring.

If there is one season of the year that exemplifies joy, it's got to be springtime. Beauty surrounds us at every turn, reminding us of God's love. The birds even seem to be singing His praises as they welcome in this new season. The grass begins to peek through the winter-hardened ground and new green blades wave their arms in thanks to the Creator. Flowers bud and bloom seemingly with little effort. And it's all for our enjoyment; it is all good and pleasing: *"God saw all that he had made, and it was very good"* **(Gen. 1:31).**

How often we take these simple pleasures of life for granted. We should be thanking God daily for our *sight* to be able to enjoy His beauty, as well the ability to be able to *hear* the birds singing their springtime melody. Sniff the fragrant flowers, and you'll be grateful for the sense of *smell*. As the earth brings forth fruits and vegetables, we should praise Him for being able to *taste*. And where would we be without the sense of *touch*?

The five senses are given to us by God so that we can enjoy His creation. Take the time to smell the roses, and as you do, thank God for all the joy He has given us in the many simple pleasures of life.

Prayer: *My heart overflows on this spring day, Lord. Thank you so much for the beauty all around. The grass as it turns green, the flowers as they bud, and the beautiful songs of the birds welcoming the new season are all reminders of Your goodness. Thank you for these blessings of joy.*

Have you had your Joy Juice today? For those of you who have spring cleaning in mind, you might need to keep that juice jug handy.

When the birds start chirping and the flowers of spring begin to peek their smiling faces toward the warm sun, many of us want to bring that freshness inside our homes. That means putting away winter clothes and giving our house a good spring cleaning. It seems over the winter months we tend to overlook some of the clutter and dirt that accumulates, but when the bright light of springtime begins to shine, we get a burst of energy, and we're ready to freshen up our homes.

Ever thought about some spring cleaning of a more personal nature? Sometimes we allow winter to set in on our spiritual lives, too. Dirt, dust, and grime build up over time, and we're not able to see things as clearly as we should. What kind of things have you allowed to clutter your spiritual home? Ask God to bring springtime into your heart and show you where you need a good spring cleaning. **1 John 1:9** says, *"If we confess our sins, he is faithful and just to forgive us our sins, and to cleanse us from all unrighteousness"* (KJV).

If you need a recommendation for a good cleanser, I would highly recommend double strength Joy Juice. Try it! I believe you'll immediately begin to see things in a brighter, more joyful light.

Prayer: *Faithful, loving Father, I ask You to cleanse me from my sins. Penetrate and permeate my thoughts and convict me of each sin as I do some spring cleaning of my own. I want my life to be a clean, clear, beautiful reflection of you. Make Your home in my heart so that I may radiate Your joy.*

Have you had your Joy Juice today? It'll help you spring into action as you face the new day.

Just as springtime gives us a renewed outlook as we breathe in the warm, fresh air, we — as children of God — should be a breath of fresh air to all those we come into contact with daily. Do you exude the fragrant aroma called the joy of the Lord?

What qualities do we need to be a person of joy — a person that's like a breath of fresh spring air?

- One who lives an authentic, genuine Christian walk has a joyful fragrance.
- A friend who *"sticketh closer than a brother"* certainly adds joy to people's lives *(Prov. 18:24,* KJV*)*.
- And most importantly, a true person of joy has a strong faith that they are willing to share with others in a loving, non-judgmental way.

Ask yourself, "Am I like a breath of fresh spring-time air, or am I still hanging onto the winter hurts and grudges that make me stale and musky?" God can do some spring cleaning in your heart, but you must first let Him in. Ask Him to replace all the clutter from the past with the springtime freshness of authenticity, unconditional love, and a strong, pure faith. You'll be in awe of how much joy will flood your heart when it's cleansed and polished by the Master Spring Cleaner.

Prayer: *Each morning with You, Jesus, is like a breath of fresh air. Your mercies are new every morning. Great is thy faithfulness! May I never tire of this truth or take for granted Your goodness and grace. Fill me with joy so that I may be bold in telling others about You.*

Have you had your Joy Juice today? Look out your window as you are sipping your juice, and see if you notice any butterflies coming your way.

Butterflies are one of the beautiful signs of springtime. Ever wonder why God created them? Is it simply for our enjoyment and pleasure? I recently read on article that said, "Humans need butterflies. Often unnoticed, they pollinate wild plants and our crops, ensuring the production of seeds and fruits required for the continued survival of plants and animals, including humans." [1] Not only are they beautiful, God created them for a purpose.

A young butterfly is a caterpillar—not very pretty. But through the process of metamorphosis, he is transformed into a beautiful creature. We humans begin life on earth as a sinful "caterpillar"—not very pretty spiritually. But if we allow God to take control of our lives, we will go through a metamorphosis of sorts and be transformed into a beautiful creature in Him: *"Therefore, if anyone is in Christ, he is a new creation; the old has gone, the new has come!"* (**2 Cor. 5:17**).

Like the butterfly, we too have a purpose: to glorify God in all that we do. Ask Him to show you your specific, unique steps to becoming the joyful creation that He intends for you to be.

Prayer: *Heavenly Creator of all beautiful things, I realize that I am nothing but a sinful caterpillar. But I have hope in You. Take me, just as I am, and change me into a beautiful butterfly, ready to share Your joy with all.*

Chapter Eight

Mama Mia!
Now, that's Some Tasty
Joy Juice!

❧

(A Special batch of Joy Juice for the week of
Mother's Day)

Have you had your Joy Juice today? If you are a Mother, pour yourself an extra serving and get ready to celebrate your special day.

Mother's Day is rapidly approaching. It's interesting how this special day originated. Back in 1908 Ana Jarvis, from Grafton, West Virginia, began a campaign to establish a national holiday called Mother's Day. Ana persuaded her mother's church in Grafton to celebrate the first Mother's Day on the anniversary of her mother's death. A memorial service was held there on May 10, 1908 and then in Philadelphia (where Ana had moved) the following year.

She and several others wanted the day to be observed by all people in the United States, so they began a letter-writing campaign to ministers, businessmen, and politicians. They were successful. In 1914, President Woodrow Wilson made the official announcement proclaiming Mother's Day a national observance that was to be held each year on the second Sunday of May. [1]

That was almost one hundred years ago, and we're still observing that special day. And rightly so! I can't think of a more deserving person to honor than my sweet mother. I'm sure many of you feel exactly the same way. Scripture tells us in **Exodus 20:12** to *"Honor your father and your mother, so that you may live long in the land the LORD your God is giving you."*

If you are blessed to still have your mother, take the time to express your love for her today. Honoring your mother not only brings joy to her but will also bring joy to your life and set a godly example for those around you.

Prayer: *I praise you, Lord, for mothers—especially godly mothers. They are a beautiful example of Your love and joy.*

Have you had your Joy Juice today? Find a deserving lady, and share a large serving with her in honor of Mother's Day. The way I see it, mothering is a ministry. It's much more than a job or a responsibility. If you are blessed to be a mother, remember that God has gifted you with your children. Do you realize what an important privilege that is? Indeed, it is a ministry. Though it is rewarding, no one can deny that it takes a lot of hard work and many sacrifices. No two children are alike, but God made mothers to somehow know how to take care of the all the intricate needs of each of her children. The Women's Study Bible gives a great explanation:

When Isaiah the prophet searched for an illustration of God's constant love for His people, the best example he could find was a new baby's mother (in Isaiah 49:15) Mothers have an enduring love. . .even in the most trying circumstances. As a mother lets go of her own life for the sake of her child, she is reminded of the depth and height and breath of God's love for her, and in a unique way she experiences the true joy of motherhood. [2]

Take a few minutes to think of all the sacrifices your own mother made for you. She did so because of her love for you. Praise the Lord for mothers, for they have instilled in us the gifts of love and knowledge; they have given us values and lots of joy.

Prayer: *Father, I thank you for creating mothers. Their enduring love is such a gift. Please forgive me for the many times that I have taken this for granted. Help me to express my love in such a way that would honor my mother and all those who take their role of Mother seriously. Show me how to share Your joy with some special mothers today.*

Have you had your Joy Juice today? Enjoy your juice this morning as we recall some of the godly mothers of the Bible.

- In Genesis we learn about Hagar, who wandered in the wilderness, crying for her child; God responded to the cry of her heart by revealing a well of water nearby to quench their thirst. (Genesis 16)
- In Exodus, we read about Jochebed who defied Pharaoh in order to save the life of her son, Moses. (Exodus 2)
- In 1 Kings you may remember the mother who appealed to Solomon and was willing to let another woman have her child rather than see the child killed. (1 Kings 3)
- In 1 Samuel, Hannah was devoted to her son, yet she willingly offered him to the Lord. (1 Samuel 1)
- And then, of course, there was Mary, Mother of Jesus.

All of these women were good mothers who loved their children unconditionally. But not all the women of the Bible were good. Likewise, in our world today there are some extremely good mothers and some not so good mothers. We must remember that God has a plan for mothers. The high calling of motherhood is an all-consuming task—twenty-four hours a day, seven days a week—for years. But, oh, the rewards are worth it.

Proverbs 31:28 says, *"Her children arise and call her blessed."* Moms, this should be our heart's desire; we should strive to live such a godly life before our children that they will one day call us a Proverbs 31 mother. Yes, that will be a joyful day.

Prayer for mothers: *Dear God, oh, how I desire to be a godly mother. So often I fall short, especially when I'm tired and overwhelmed with all the responsibilities of my family. Will you please give me strength and wisdom to take one day at a time, relying on You to help me with each decision? Beginning now, help me to draw closer and closer toward You and toward becoming that Proverbs 31 woman. Fill my heart with Your joy so that I may spill over onto my family members.*

Have you had your Joy Juice today? When Mama serves it, it tastes extra sweet.

Mothers have that special touch, don't they? When a little one falls and scrapes a knee or bumps a head, to whom do they go running for comfort? Mama. If they're feeling sick or get their feelings hurt, no one can soothe them like the loving arms of their mommy. Mothers have such a great impact on the lives of their children (as do fathers). But often we get so busy with the *urgent* that we forget what is truly *important*.

Parents, I challenge you to remember what the Word of God says in

Deuteronomy 11:18, 19: *"Fix these words of mine in your hearts and minds. . . Teach them to your children, talking about them when you sit at home and when you walk along the road, when you lie down and when you get up."* Every day is a new opportunity to teach our children the important truths about God. What a privilege to mold young lives in such a positive way.

Mothers, this Sunday we will celebrate you. Ask God to help you be a godly mother, making you aware of opportunities throughout each day to share His love. Grandmothers, aunts, sisters, friends, you too are an important tool that God can use to direct the path of the children He has put in your life. Let's accept our role with exceeding, abundant joy.

Prayer: *May I take advantage of every opportunity, Lord, that You give me to teach the children about You. As we sit at home, give me wisdom to turn off the television and talk to the children about how to have a relationship with You. As we drive to school or to events or to the grocery store, open doors for discussion that will be teachable moments. Use me in these young lives to lead them to depend on You. It is my desire and prayer that they have Your joy in their hearts for a lifetime.*

Have you had your Joy Juice today? If you don't have your Mother's Day gift picked out, may I suggest a case of joy juice tied with a pink ribbon?

So much could be said about the dear women that God has placed in our lives. Our mother is often our teacher, our advisor, and our encourager; she is one who inspires. T. DeWitt Talmage said it best when he said, "A mother is the bank where we deposit all our hurts and worries." [3] I agree, but I'd add that we also deposit with her our hopes and dreams.

There's an old Jewish proverb that says, "A mother understands what a child does not say." [4] How true! Mothers deserve our honor, praise, and gratitude for so many reasons. This Sunday is Mother's Day. Do you have plans to honor your mother? May I make a few suggestions?

- One of the best ways to honor your mother is to worship our Lord. If possible, attend church with your mom.
- Write her a card or letter telling her how much you love her, and list some of the reasons why.
- Give her an extra long hug. That gift fits any budget. Very few mothers ever tire of feeling

the arms of their children wrapped tightly around them in love.

- If your mother has passed on, do something in her memory. Perhaps you could make a donation to a project at her church or donate a book in her memory to your local library.

Take the time to thank God for all the special ladies in your life. To my mom, I'd like to joyfully dedicate **Proverbs 31:29**: *"Many women do noble things, but you surpass them all."* Happy Mother's Day, Mama! I love you!

Prayer: *Dear Father, thank you for my mother. Thank you for the joy she has exhibited through the years. I praise You for her example and her unconditional love. You have blessed my life with joy by using the beautiful vessel that I lovingly call "My Mother."*

Chapter Nine

All Natural Joy Juice Smoothies

Have you had your Joy Juice today? Be a good example to others, and drink it daily.

In her book *Having a Mary Heart in a Martha World*, Joanna Weaver gives a clear illustration of what kind of example we should strive to be:

"The story is told of a young boy who approached an evangelist after a revival meeting one night. 'Excuse me, sir?' the little boy said politely. 'You said everyone should ask Jesus into their hearts, right?'

'That's right, son.' The minister squatted down so he could look the boy in the eye.

'Did you ask him in?'

'Well, I'd like to,' the boy said, 'but I got to figurin'. . .I'm so little and Jesus is so big—he's just gonna stick out all over!'

'That's the point, son,' the man said with a smile, 'that's the point.'" [1]

Does Jesus "stick out all over" in your life? Do others see Him when they look at you? It should be our heart's desire to be so much like Jesus that people have no doubt that we're Christians.

Romans 8:29 teaches us that it's God's plan for us to be like Jesus, "*...to be conformed to the likeness of his Son.*" Are you willing to allow Him to have complete control of your life? Ask God for the boldness to take a stand for Him and to reflect Jesus with your words, your actions, and your attitude. When you make that decision, you will be setting a genuine, godly example for all those around you, and you will be pouring out the joy of the Lord onto their lives. An immediate reward will be that the joy will bounce right back to you.

Prayer: *Jesus, help me to be an authentic Christian. When people look at me, let them see you "sticking out all over" in every area of my life. I desire to be so like You that my words will be what You would say. I want the places that I go to be the places You would choose to go, and I want my reactions to reflect how You would react. Help me to become a pure, natural, beautiful reflection of joy because of my relationship with You.*

Have you had your Joy Juice today? If you want to be a genuine, joyful example, help yourself to a huge serving.

What kind of role model are you setting for those who are watching your example? You do realize that people are watching you, don't you? Whether it's a child who looks up to you or a coworker who is working along side of you...people are looking. And many times, the people we don't even realize are watching are the most influenced by our reactions and decisions.

Do you remember the old hymn entitled "Let Others See Jesus in You?" Take the time to read these beautiful words and let them penetrate your heart:

While passing thro' this world of sin/and others your life shall view,
Be clean and pure without, within/Let others see Jesus in you.

Your life's a book before their eyes/ They're reading it thro' and thro',
Say, does it point them to the skies/ Do others see Jesus in you?

What joy 'twill be at set of sun/ In mansions beyond the blue,
To find some souls that you have won/ Let others see Jesus in you.

Then live for Christ both day and night/ Be faithful, be brave, and true,
And lead the lost to life and light/ Let others see Jesus in you.

Chorus:
Let others see Jesus in you, Let others see Jesus in you;
Keep telling the story, be faithful and true, Let others see Jesus in you. [2]

If we profess to be a Christian, then we ought to reflect Christ. In our behavior and in our devotion to God, we are to be like Jesus. The way we dress, the way we talk, the music we listen to, the people we hang out with—all of these are areas in our life that demonstrate whether we are serious about becoming like Him.

Be an authentic example of joy in someone's life today.

Prayer: *My simple prayer today is "Let others see Jesus in me!"*

Have you had your Joy Juice today? Hope you got up on the right side of the bed this morning and are approaching your day with the joyful attitude of Christ.

Let's just imagine what this world would be like if we all had the attitude of Jesus. There would be no one demanding their rights. We would all be putting others' needs before our own. There would be peace and harmony throughout the world.

Philippians 2:5-7 explains, *"Your attitude should be the same as that of Christ Jesus: Who, being in very nature God, did not consider equality with God something to be grasped, but made himself nothing, taking the very nature of a servant, being made in human likeness."*

What an example! Jesus was willing to give up his rights as the Son of God in order to be obedient and serve. For many people, the word *servant* holds negative connotations. In the Christian context, a servant is one who is willing to become like Christ— and that's a good thing.

Let's put ourselves under the microscope and examine our attitudes, our lifestyle, and our goals. What are you like *au naturale* spiritually? Are you Christ-like in every area of your life? If not, come clean before God, and ask Him to help you be aware of the germs of selfishness, pride, and evil behavior. When we allow Him to transform our lives, we will be ready to set a joyful, spiritually healthy example before others.

Prayer: *Dear God, take the blinders from my eyes, and help me to see my spiritual condition for what it truly is. Give me wisdom to see the areas that I am holding on to so tightly. Give me the courage and discipline to let go and let You take control. Change my heart so that my attitude can genuinely be like Yours. I want to be a representation of You and Your joy.*

Have you had your Joy Juice today? Be careful how you answer that question.

We're not always careful about the words that come from our mouths, are we? We'd like to set a good example, but do we always succeed? Some people are in the habit of using profanity. They've become so desensitized that they don't even realize how often the words pass through their lips.

The Bible is very plain about this subject: *"Let no unwholesome word proceed from your mouth, but only such a word as is good for edification according to the need of the moment, so that it will give grace to those who hear"* (Eph. 4:29 NASB).

Do your words give grace to those who hear? Are they helpful for building others up? You may be thinking, "My words are not really awful, just slang. And it helps me to fit in so that I can witness better to those of my friends who don't know Christ." Well, as writer Steve Hall puts it, "That's like saying I need to go rob a bank so I can lead bank robbers to the Lord. Or I need to kill somebody so I can lead murderers to the Lord. The Bible emphasizes the need for Christians to speak with a consistent mouth." [3]

"Out of the same mouth proceedeth blessing and cursing. My brethren, these things ought not so to be" (**James 3:10** KJV).

Be intentional about listening to the words which come from your own mouth. Many times we are quick to judge others and can see where they are going wrong, but we are blind to our own faults. So listen to yourself, and determine if all your words are edifying and full of grace and joy.

Prayer: *Father, please take hold of my heart and tongue with such a firm grasp that I am keenly aware of the example I am setting before others. Light a fire in me to be diligent and intentional in walking and talking the joy of the Lord.*

Have you had your Joy Juice today? Set a good example for your family by being consistent.

Those of you who deal with children realize the importance of consistency. Children need to know what is expected. They need to know their boundaries. Watch toddlers as they begin to explore. It's not easy for them. They have just discovered they can make choices, and they've become quite mobile. They have no concept of danger or fear, so some of their choices can be dangerous, even fatal. They need help in making good choices so they can learn what is safe, as well as what is acceptable, in a wide range of situations.

The same is true of us in the spiritual context. We are like toddlers, exploring our boundaries. It's not always an easy road. Though some of our decisions are common sense choices, others are extremely difficult. At times we rush into things and make impulsive decisions that leave us hurting and embarrassed.

Psalm 46:1 tells us, *"God is our refuge and strength, an ever-present help in trouble."* No matter what our age, we can depend on God. Regardless of our spiritual maturity level, we all need His help, His strength, His protection, and His guidance. When we grow up in the Lord, we will learn that we can call on him at any time. Like the toddler, we can lift our arms to our Father, and He will pick us up and carry us, helping us to make good, consistent choices which will lead to joy.

Prayer: *Heavenly Father, I am so child-like in many ways. I lack wisdom, experience, and knowledge in numerous situations that I face daily. Please be with me, teach me, guide me, and protect me. Help me to lean more heavily on You for You are my refuge, my strength, and my joy.*

Have you had your Joy Juice today? It's the real thing. Are you?

When people look at you, do they see someone who is genuine, transparent, and real? I'm afraid that many times we put on our masks, and we show others only what we want them to see. We may be able to fool people, but God sees the real us. I'm sure that many times I disappoint Him by saying one thing, yet doing another: by teaching a Sunday School lesson on Sunday and not living it out during the week; by telling you to be patient and then losing my cool. Do you know what that's called? It's called being a hypocrite.

None of us want to be called *that!* The sad truth is that we all fall into that category at one time or another. Beth Moore says sometimes it's easier to act than clean up our act. Do you ever find yourself pretending that everything is rosy, but on the inside you are hurting, anxious, angry, bitter, and depressed? This is when we put on our happy face and say all the right things because we don't want people to know the truth. That, my friend, is being hypocritical.

What's the remedy for this spiritual condition called hypocrisy? A steady diet of joy juice, which is filled with spiritual nutrients and reminds us that

God loves us. When we accept our real value in Him, we can be the real thing. He loves us and wants us to love each other sincerely. *"**Let love be genuine**,"* Paul teaches in **Romans 12:9** (ESV).

So, take a huge gulp of your natural Joy Juice smoothie right now. It'll give you strength to face whatever may come your way with a genuine heart of gratitude, love, and joy.

Prayer: *Remove my mask, Lord, and let me be real and genuine. If You can love me even when I'm unlovable, then help me to love myself enough to let the truth shine through. Shine Your love on me, in me, through me, and around me. Thank you, Jesus. I'm already feeling more joyful.*

Have you had your Joy Juice today? It sure helps when you're trying to balance all that life brings your way.

Our life is full of obligations, responsibilities, and opportunities. Sometimes we feel very overwhelmed by it all. If we're not careful, we can stay so busy doing good things that we miss out on the best things. Often we get so burdened with the urgent that we allow it to affect our health.

Are you consumed with work? Do you spend more time thinking, planning, and carrying out duties on the job than you do attending to your family's needs? Are you so into a hobby that you neglect the responsibilities of your job, your spouse, and your children? Or on the opposite end of the pendulum, do you obsess over your family so much that you exclude everyone and everything else?

My point is that we *need* balance. We should work hard, yes, doing everything as unto the Lord as the scripture instructs. But we also need to make time for God, family, and much-needed rest.

In his sermon "Listening to Jesus in a Noisy World, Bernie Cueto uses the following illustration:

"The story is told of a man who challenged another guy to an all-day wood

chopping contest. The challenger worked very hard, stopping only for a brief lunch

break. The other man had a leisurely lunch and took several breaks during the day.

At the end of the day, the challenger was surprised and annoyed to find that the other

fellow had chopped substantially more wood than he had. 'I don't get it,' he said.

'Every time I checked, you were taking a rest, yet you chopped more wood than I

did.'

'But you didn't notice,' said the winning woodsman, 'that I was sharpening my

ax when I sat down to rest.'" [4]

Take an honest assessment of your busy life. Are you in balance? God will help you to prioritize so that you'll know when it's time to "sharpen your ax" while resting. Your life will be much more joyful when it's balanced according to God's scales.

"Love the Lord your God with all your heart and with all your soul and with all your mind and with all your strength." **Mark 13:30**

Prayer: *Remind me often, Father, that I cannot accomplish Your best if I am stretched beyond my limits. I am so thankful that You are limit**less**. May I trust in You to show me how to balance my life in such a way that I exemplify a genuine love and joy that can come only from You.*

Have you had your Joy Juice today? I'm glad you have, but remember to eat a balanced diet along with that juice.

There once was a little boy who loved ice cream. He asked for ice cream at every meal. But his mother and father always insisted that he eat a balanced meal before he got the ice cream. One night the little boy was fussing and complaining so much about having to eat his vegetables that his parents decided on an alternative plan of action. The dad said, "Son, would you be happy if we let you eat ice cream for every meal?" The boy was somewhat surprised by his dad's question, but quickly answered "Yes!" "Okay," responded the father with a twinkle in his eye.

And that's exactly what the parents did. For each meal, they scooped a bowl of ice cream for the boy and set it at his plate. The first couple of meals were delightful for the little boy, but soon he started asking for other foods. "No," the parents said. "We're giving you what you asked for." After several meals, the boy would not even touch his ice cream; he began to cry for real, healthy food. He admitted to his father and mother that they knew best and that he would trust them from now on.

Does this story sound familiar, spiritually speaking? We think we know what's best for us without consulting our Heavenly Father. We want all the ice cream without having to eat the yucky vegetables. But God knows that we need balance in our lives—the struggles as well as the good times. That's what shapes our faith and helps us to grow into spiritually healthy, mature Christians who can have joy regardless of our circumstances. Always remember the joyful truth found in **Philippians 4:19:** *"And my God will supply all your needs according to His riches in glory in Christ Jesus."*

Prayer: *Father, I understand that You know what is best for me. But I confess that many times I find myself telling You what I "need." Please help me to turn loose and allow You to be in control so that my life will be balanced with what You have intended. However, I'd be more than happy to take an overload of Your joy.*

Have you had your Joy Juice today? Drink it whether you're feeling up or down.

I have vivid memories of playing on the seesaws at recess in elementary school. I liked playing with someone my own size so that the ride would be smooth and balanced. Occasionally, I'd pair up with someone bigger than I was, and I'd end up in the air a whole lot longer that I wanted to be. I wasn't especially fond of heights. But I learned one day that if I'd get someone to ride with me on my side of the seesaw, we could balance out that heavier friend on the other side.

That might have been one of my first good lessons on the value of friendship and balancing life's challenges. Have you noticed that God places certain people in your life right when you need them the most? Sometimes the seesaw of life puts you up in the air, and you don't know how you're going to get down. Then God sends a friend to ride with you.

Sometimes you may be so frightened by the "height" of the situation that you can only close your eyes and hang on tight. But your friend is able to see things more clearly and advise you when to let go. At times, you may be paralyzed with fear and cannot even pray, but this friend will intercede and pray for you: *"A man of many companions may come to ruin, but there is a friend who sticks closer than a brother"* (Prov. 18:24).

What a treasure a true friend can be! But be careful not to abuse the friendship by holding on so tight that they can't breathe. Remember, it's all about balance. The only Friend that never gets tired of our holding tight is our best friend, Jesus. He considers it a joy to ride with us on the seesaw of life.

Prayer: *Father, in many ways, life is like a seesaw. Thank you for riding with me, no matter what. There are several friends who come to mind that I am sure You sent to me at certain points of my life. My heart is full of gratitude and joy because they are such an important part of my life. Today I pray a special prayer for each of them:*

Have you had your Joy Juice today? It's a great tonic to help you with your balance.

Imagine yourself sixty to seventy feet above the ground on a platform as thousands of faces watch and wait for you to balance yourself and walk across a thin wire only a 1/2-inch thick. That's the reality of the world of high wire acrobatics. Performers must have much training and many years of practice before mastering the feat of high wire walking.

Some of us feel as if that's what we are doing many days in this circus called life—a balancing act. We try to balance our schedules between family, job, school, church, friends, civic responsibilities, doctor's appointments, weddings, funerals, projects, and occasionally, rest and relaxation. Our list could go on and on, but the fact is that frequently we have too many "acts" on our agenda and not enough time to perform them skillfully. Plainly put, we're just out of balance.

In this circus called life, we need to allow God to be our Ring Master. He will direct us to the ring or act that needs our immediate attention. **(Psalm 73:24:** *You guide me with your counsel, and afterward you will take me into glory.")* If we will listen to Him, he will help us to prioritize and put balance in our lives.

There will be clowns that come along who will entertain us, and it's great to laugh and enjoy life along the way. But we don't need to get so distracted with all the fun that we forget what is truly important: staying in the center ring called His will. That's where we will find true joy.

Prayer: *Whew! Lord, I do feel so stressed many days with the many activities, responsibilities, and choices that I make to stay busy. Help me to see which ones are truly important and then let the others go. Give me balance by helping me to go to You before every decision. Then give me the resolve to follow Your instructions. I ask for a double serving of Joy Juice today to balance out any challenges that the enemy may try to send my way.*

Have you had your Joy Juice today? Drinking your share will help you to become a spiritual Olympian.

I love watching the Olympics, both Summer and Winter. The games are a culmination of years of sacrifice and training. The athletes spend hours, days, weeks, and years concentrating on the skills of their sport with the goal of becoming one of the best in the world. But I've noticed that regardless of their sport, one skill is always necessary—balance.

If runners or skaters can't stay balanced on their feet, they'll trip themselves up and fall. If gymnasts are unable to balance themselves on the beam or the high bars, they'll loose their grip and crash to the floor. Divers need balance as they climb the ladder and stand on the board to make that high dive. Each competitor needs the gift of balance in order to do their best.

We, too, are like those athletes, competing in the Olympics of Life. In order to succeed and perform our best, we need balance. We need to prioritize and continually take inventory of what's on our list of things to do today. What's top of your list? If it's not God, then you need to start a new list. God should always be our top priority. If He's first, He will fill you with wisdom as to how to balance the other important things in your life.

So in this race called life, let us do as **Hebrews 12:1** says, "*...throw off everything that hinders and the sin that so easily entangles, and let us run with perseverance the race marked out for us.*" Run with joy so that you will complete the race as a champion.

Prayer: How often I feel like I am in a race, Father. I am racing here and there with no specific goal in mind. Help me to set godly goals for myself and may they be inspired by You. Show me how to get rid of all that hinders me from winning the race of joy.

Chapter Ten

Concentrated Joy Juice Squeezed from God's Word

Have you had your Joy Juice today? Sip and see that it is good. If you will read from the book of Psalms, you'll find reason after reason to be joyful.

Pick up your Bible, and turn to the center; there you'll find the book of Psalms. This book is a beautiful collection of prayers and songs. David and the other writers openly and unashamedly pour out their true feelings. When we read attentively, we will notice that their words reflect a deep love for God and a life-changing relationship with Him. As the notes in my Life Application Bible explain: "The Psalmists confess their sins, express their doubts and fears, ask God for help in times of trouble, and they praise and worship him." [1]

Today let's talk about praise. Psalms includes many songs of praise to God as our Creator, our Sustainer, and our Redeemer. Do you know what praise is? It's recognizing, appreciating, and expressing God's greatness. Focusing our thoughts on God is so important because it moves us to want to praise Him. The more we know him, the closer we will draw to Him, and the more we can appreciate what He has done for us. This awareness fills our hearts with joy and gratitude, which leads to praise.

"*Shout for joy to the LORD, all the earth,*" **Psalm 100** instructs.

As we go along our way today, let's focus on God and His greatness. Before we know it, we may be singing a song of joyful praise.

Prayer: *Almighty, Wonderful Counselor! Precious, loving Savior! I praise Your Holy and Righteous Name! I sing of Your greatness and goodness. Oh, how You fill my heart with joy. May I praise You all day—and tonight in my sleep, as well. Hide in my heart so that I may forever be joyful.*

Have you had your Joy Juice today? You forgot? Well, I forgive you.

Speaking of forgiving, the book of Psalms contains many intense prayers asking God for forgiveness. One such prayer is found in **Psalm 86:3-5**: *"Have mercy on me, O Lord, for I call to you all day long. Bring joy to your servant, for to you, O Lord, I lift up my soul. You are forgiving and good, O Lord, abounding in love to all who call to you."*

Every one of us has done things for which we need forgiveness, don't you agree? We have made poor choices that have hurt others; we have broken God's commandments; we have been disobedient. Without God's forgiveness, our lives will be miserable—the opposite of joyful.

Not long ago I was setting up tables for an event at our church, and I noticed that some of the tables had marks and stains on them. Instead of panicking or fretting, I had a plan. I set out to find some of the prettiest, most colorful table cloths possible and placed them on the tables to cover the ugly spots. I then put an attractive centerpiece on each table. During the event, not one person noticed the ugly, marred tables because all they could see were the pretty tablecloths and decorations. That's the way it is with our sins.

God covers them if we ask Him. When we are truly repentant, God will place a beautiful table cloth of forgiveness on our life, complete with a centerpiece of love.

As **Psalm 103:12** tells us, *"as far as the east is from the west, so far has he removed our transgressions from us."* God's great love, mercy, and grace will fill us with joy.

Prayer: *Thank you, dear Father, for forgiving all my transgressions. How many times have I failed You, yet You continue to extend Your mercy and compassion! You bring joy to my soul as You lift me up. Please read my grateful heart. Help me to be more like You—forgiving others as You have forgiven me.*

Have you had your Joy Juice today? You'll be thankful you did.

The beautiful book of Psalms frequently addresses the subject of thankfulness. Look at the passage in **Psalm 118**. This chapter begins and ends with the same words: *"Give thanks to the LORD, for he is good; his love endures forever."* God's love is unchanging in the midst of changing circumstances. This should give us a sense of security and peace. And isn't that what everyone is searching for today—peace?

We have so much for which to be thankful. God has a personal interest in each one of us. Not only does He protect, guide, and forgive us, but He is also our Provider, our Comforter, and our Rock of Salvation.

How often do you thank God? Is it something that you do regularly? Or do you take for granted many of the blessings that He continually pours out on you? If we're not careful, we will focus on the things we don't have instead of all the things that we do. God knows us better than we know ourselves and that includes what we truly *need*. Do you trust Him completely to satisfy those needs in His perfect timing?

Here's a joyful reminder that will help you to live an abundant life: *"Give thanks to the LORD, for he is good; his love endures forever!"*

Prayer: *Dear Lord, I admit that I often take my blessings for granted. You have been so generous with Your unconditional love, provision, protection, and so much more. Help me to remember how blessed I am when I start complaining about what I don't have. May my focus be on You because You are all I need. Thank You for the joyful gift of You.*

Have you had your Joy Juice today? Trust me; it's really good for you.

Do you find it difficult to trust? You may if you've been hurt by someone in the past. But the wonderful thing about being a Christian is knowing that we can rest in the truth that...in contrast to people...God can always be trusted. Over and over again in the book of Psalms, the writers encourage us with verses reminding us to trust in God.

Psalm 33:21 (KJV) says, *"For our heart shall rejoice in Him, because we have trusted in his holy name."* Did you get that? Our heart shall rejoice, why? Because we have trusted in His Holy Name. And then **Psalm 2:12** (KJV) says, *"Blessed are all they that put their trust in him."*

Do you want to be blessed? Do you want to experience joy? I certainly do. Then, we must trust in him. No one can do it for us; this is a decision we must each make—individually. In Oswald Chamber's book *Bringing Sons to Glory* he wrote, "No one can tell us where the shadow of the Almighty is, we have to find it out for ourselves. When by obedience we have discovered where it is, we must abide there— 'no evil shall befall you, nor shall any plague come near your dwelling.' That is the life that is more than conquerors because the joy of the Lord has become its strength, and that soul is on the way to entering ultimately into the joy of the Lord." [2]

When we trust Him completely, the joy of the Lord becomes our strength.

Prayer: *Lord, it is such a relief to know that I can trust You. Never, even for a split second, do I have to wonder if You're going to do what You say in Your Word. Trust is a quality I don't see a lot of these days. Often I come into contact with people who don't keep their word. Some betray their closest friends. But I am grateful beyond expression that I will never have to worry about Your trustworthiness. Indeed, my heart rejoices because of my trust in You.*

Have you had your Joy Juice today? Are you wide awake? A serving of Joy Juice always helps to get you ready to face the day.

When you wake up each morning, what's the first thing that comes to your mind? Is it the list of things you've got to do today? Or maybe you begin to worry about what *might* happen. It could be that you find yourself immediately nursing the hurts from yesterday.

What a difference we would experience if the first thoughts we had each day were thoughts of joyful praise and gratitude. **Psalm 68:3** says, *"But may the righteous be glad/ and rejoice before God; may they be happy and joyful."* If we get into the habit of waking up to each new day with a prayer of gratitude before the Lord, then our hearts will be much better prepared for what the day might bring.

For the next few mornings, as soon as you awaken, before climbing out of bed, try thanking God for several things. Your list will be different from anyone else's. But one thing's for sure, we all have many blessings for which to be thankful. If you will start your day today (and the next few mornings) with praise to the Lord, it won't be long before you'll be smiling more and complaining less. Hopefully, this will be the start of a lifelong habit, a habit that will be joyfully contagious.

Prayer: *Thank you, thank you, thank you, Father, for my many blessings. Indeed, I am abundantly blessed. First of all, I want to thank You for sending Jesus to die for me. Next, I thank You for having a relationship with me and demonstrating Your constant and abiding love. And here's my personal list of things I want to express my gratitude for today:* _____ _____.

Have you had your Joy Juice today? Start your day off right with a large serving. There's just something about beginning your day with a joy boost.

As you begin each morning, do you look forward to the opportunities that may come your way? Or do you find yourself dreading what *might* happen? Many times, as we arise and ready ourselves for the day, we find ourselves under the cloud of yesterday. We recall the careless words of someone who hurt us; we worry about the doctor's report that we're expecting; we stress over situations involving our children. There are days when the last thing we want to do is rejoice.

But listen to the words of the psalmist in **Psalm 118:24**: *"This is the day the LORD has made; let us rejoice and be glad in it."* "Let us rejoice"—it's as if the writer is reminding us that we have a choice. We can choose to expect the worst to happen, or we can praise the Lord for a new day and face it with a joyful attitude.

God has given us this new day to live and to serve him. Be glad!

Prayer: *Sweet Jesus, I choose to be joyful today. I know that things may come my way that will be challenging, but in Your strength, I will rejoice—regardless of my circumstances.*

Have you had your Joy Juice today? I'm soooo glad you did.

In **Psalm 16:9** David wrote, *"My heart is glad and my tongue rejoices."* Have you ever thought about what it means to have a glad heart? Is it the feeling that we get when we buy a new car? Or when we find just the right outfit for that important event? Or maybe it's when we get to take that vacation that we have excitedly anticipated for a long time.

Sure, those things are nice, but are they truly what make our heart glad? How long is that car going to stay brand new? And how long will it take for that outfit to go out of style? I can promise you, the memories of that trip will fade. (This grandma knows what she's talking about.)

The secret of a glad heart is much more than mere happiness. Happiness is temporary because it's based on our circumstances. But true joy is lasting because it's based on God's presence within us. If you have asked Jesus into your heart and you are living for Him, then you know exactly what David meant by his words: *"My heart is glad and my tongue rejoices!"*

Prayer: *Oh, Father, how my heart rejoices because I have you. May every word that comes from my mouth be a testimony of Your goodness, mercy, and joy.*

Have you had your Joy Juice today? Sometimes I need an extra serving when things happen that I don't understand.

In the past few months, there have been several situations that occurred in the lives of my friends and acquaintances that I truly do not understand. Tragic accidents have claimed productive, young lives; a couple lost two of their children within six months of one another; a godly woman who has always served the Lord was diagnosed with a terminal disease. These circumstances are beyond my understanding.

Have you ever asked the question, "Why does God allow bad things to happen to good people?" This is one of the most difficult questions in all of theology. And there is no simple answer. We must acknowledge that God is eternal, all-knowing, and faithful. And His ways are *"higher than our ways."* **(Isaiah 55:9)**

You'll recall in the book of Job that God allowed Satan to do everything he wanted to Job, except kill him. He took away his family, his possessions, and his health. Do you remember Job's reaction? *"Though he slay me, yet will I hope in him"* **(Job 13:15)**. And, he further said, *"The LORD gave and the LORD has taken away; may the name of the*

LORD be praised" **(Job 1:21).** Job didn't understand *why* God allowed these things to happen, but he knew God was good. Therefore, he continued to trust in Him.

When difficult times come upon us, is our reaction like that of Job? Only when we possess this kind of unwavering love for God will we be able to experience joy in all things.

Prayer: *I confess, dear Lord, that there are some things I truly do not understand. Help me to see that I am not supposed to understand it all, but I must simple trust you in all things. May my faith grow to be strong like Job's. Let me feel Your arms of protection and comfort around me no matter what my circumstances. Please fill me with joy in all things.*

Have you had your Joy Juice today? Are you going through a troubling time? Keep on drinking your Joy Juice. You'll need every drop.

Do you know what often happens when we take our eyes off of Jesus and begin to focus on our problems? We forget to drink our Joy Juice, and we try to take matters into our own hands. Sometimes we give up on God—and even get angry with Him. Many people think that because they make a decision to follow Christ they should be exempt from trouble. When problems arise, they begin to question why God would allow the circumstance to happen. That's when we need to go to the book of Job and read what he went through, never forsaking His faith.

The footnote in my Life Application Bible challenges us:

"The message of Job is that we should not give up on God…especially in the midst of difficult circumstances. Faith in God does not guarantee personal prosperity, just as lack of faith does not guarantee troubles. If this were so, people would believe in God simply to get rich. God is capable of rescuing us from suffering, but he may also allow suffering to come for reasons we cannot understand." [3]

When we find ourselves questioning why God has allowed certain things to happen, we need to go back to our powerful verse in **Proverbs 3:5:** *"Trust in the LORD with all your heart, and lean not on your own understanding."* When we put our complete trust in Him, we will be able to quit trying to figure out all the *whys*. Instead, let's put the problems in His hands and say, *"Not my will but thine be done."* **(Luke 22:42)**

Now, sit back and practice joy in ALL things.

Prayer: *Thank you, Lord, that I can always depend on You. Give me perseverance when I most need it. Help me never to give up on You, even when I don't see an answer to my calamity. May my faith be strong enough to always give You glory and honor, as well as "count it all joy." (James 1:2 KJV)*

Have you had your Joy Juice today? It will help you to remember to practice.

School children have to practice their ABC's, counting, multiplication tables, and writing skills. Musicians have to practice their instruments, and athletes practice their sport. The only way to improve our skills is to practice. Do you think Venus and Serena Williams ever practice their tennis skills? They must practice for countless hours, to be sure. That dedication is what makes both of them Wimbledon champions.

The Dove Award winning artist Cheri Keaggy practices more than just her music. There's a song that Cheri has written that expresses exactly why she can sing about the joy of the Lord, regardless of the circumstances of her life. The song entitled "Restored" says that we all have times of testing in our lives. There will be times when we feel as if we are "living against the grindstone." But it's at these times *especially* that we need to practice joy.

Read the beautiful lyrics Cheri has written:

I've been living against the grindstone, where nothing is sure but the Lord.

For He gives me the treasures of darkness,
where faith's greatest riches are stored.
And in ways that are quite unexpected, I
have learned a most humbling truth….
That a faith that has never been tested is just
growth that is long overdue.
So I'm practicing joy, choosing it daily, putting
it on like a favorite cologne. And when life
breaks me down, it won't even faze me.
Some call me crazy, but I'm just in love with
the Lord. [4]

Yes, if we truly love the Lord, everything takes on a new perspective. Let's practice joy, regardless of our circumstances.

Prayer: *I'm practicing joy, Lord. Remind me of that continually throughout the day. I know that I must have You to help me practice because I sure can't do it in my own strength. Thank you for the joy You so freely give. I love you and want to share that love and joy with others.*

(Cheri Keaggy's CD can be found at
www.cherikeaggy.com)

Have you had your Joy Juice today? Are you successful in remembering to drink it throughout each day?

Back in my high school days, we had a cheer that went something like this:

S-U-C-C-E-S-S, we're the BEST of all the REST! Isn't that what we're taught? We think that to be successful, we've got to be better than everyone else. Sure, competition can be healthy, and we do want to strive to be the best that God created us to be. But sometimes, we lose sight of the balance between aiming toward success and doing whatever it takes to get there—even stepping on others to accomplish our goal.

Biblical success is very different from the world's definition. In order to be a success in God's eyes, we must put others *before* ourselves. **Philippians 2:3** tells us, *"in humility consider others better than your-selves."* Selfish ambition ruins relationships; genuine humility can build others up. Our words and actions should be edifying and encouraging—always.

You see, when we let God put a guard over our mouths and allow Him to be in control of our thoughts and reactions, we can be successful. S-U-C-C-E-S-S, God's way is the very BEST!

Prayer: *My desire, Father, is to please you. Only then will I feel that I am a true success. I know I cannot do it alone, so I'm counting on You to show me the way. My goal is to see the joy of the Lord in all circumstances. That would make me feel joyfully successful.*

Have you had your Joy Juice today? Hope it tastes really good.

What is your definition of *good*? One dictionary (*thefreedictionary.com*) states that *good* means "Being positive or desirable in nature; not bad." [5] When we talk about a good book or a good movie, it's really a matter of who is giving their opinion. What might be good to me might not be good to you. Some people think raw oysters are good to eat, but that opinion is not true for me. You see, what is good is subjective to the opinion of the person doing the judging.

Let's ponder this question again: "Why do bad things happen to good people?" Maybe a better question would be, "Why does God allow good things to happen to bad people?" **Romans 5:8** declares, *"But God demonstrates his own love for us in this: While we were still sinners, Christ died for us."* Despite the sinful nature of the people of this world, God still loves us. He loved us enough to take the penalty for our sins.

Sometimes bad things happen to people who seem undeserving of them. But God allows things to happen for His reasons, whether or not we understand them. Above all, we must remember that God is loving, just, and merciful. When things happen to us that we simply cannot understand, instead of doubting God's goodness, our reaction should be to simply trust Him.

Trusting the Lord wholeheartedly leads to a life of joy.

Prayer: *Father, I know that I am not to understand Your ways because they are so much higher than mine (Isaiah 55:9). Help me to trust Your wisdom, knowing that because of Your love for me, I can depend on You for all my needs and concerns. Just resting in that truth fills my heart with joy.*

Chapter Eleven

Drink Up!
No Excuses!!

Have you had your Joy Juice today? No excuses!

All of us are guilty of coming up with excuses when we forget to do something or when we simply don't want to do it. Remember some of the excuses we used to try on our school teachers? We've all heard the "dog ate my homework" excuse. One of the best I ever heard was as follows: "I lost my homework while I was fighting with this boy who said you weren't the best teacher in the whole school."

What do you imagine God thinks when we try to give Him excuses? For instance, when we don't read our Bible and pray each day, our excuse could easily be, "It's just impossible to find the time!" God might respond by saying, *"The things which are impossible with men are possible with God"* (**Luke 18:27 KJV**). We sometimes say, "I'm too tired!" God answers, *"Come to me, all you who are weary and burdened, and I will give you rest" (Matt. 11:28).*

Making excuses started way back with Adam and Eve. Remember? Adam blamed Eve for making him eat the fruit, and then Eve blamed the serpent. I guess it's just human nature not to want to own up to our own bad choices.

When God speaks to our heart to serve Him in some way or to strive for a closer relationship with Him, instead of wasting time thinking up excuses, we need to spend our time praying and asking God to lead us one step at a time. Let's quit making excuses so that we can experience the joy of the Lord.

Prayer: *No more excuses from me, Lord. I want to live for You—whole-heartedly. Remind me daily that I can trust in You for strength, power, and wisdom. Guide me down the path of joy.*

Have you had your Joy Juice today? If not, then what's your excuse? It's easy to make excuses—like why we can't attend church or serve in some way. But, if it were something like a shopping trip or a sporting event, would we use the same excuses?

Some years ago the magazine *Moody Monthly* ran a piece which included excuses which a person might use for not going to sporting events. See if you catch the implications of these excuses:

- Every time I go, they ask for money.
- The people don't seem very friendly.
- The seats are too hard and uncomfortable.
- The coach never comes to see me.
- The referee made a decision with which I could not agree.
- The band played numbers that I had never heard before.
- My parents took me to too many games when I was growing up.
- I don't want to take my children because I want them to choose for themselves what sport they like best. [1]

You get the point? Before we make our next excuse, let's remember that God never makes excuses when we call on Him. So let's follow His example. **Romans 1:20** tells us, *"For since the creation of the world God's invisible qualities—his eternal power and divine nature—have been clearly seen. . .so that men are without excuse."*

Prayer: *God, I praise you and thank you that You never make excuses. I can trust Your Word, and I know that You will never leave me. Help me to quit making excuses for not following the Holy Spirit's prompting. Make me sensitive to Your voice, and make me always be ready to share Your joy.*

Have you had your Joy Juice today? Not yet? Are you looking for an excuse?

Sometimes our excuse is simply procrastination. Here's a pretty entertaining illustration about procrastination:

Arnold was cleaning out the attic with his wife when he came across a claim ticket from the local shoe repair shop. The date stamped on the ticket showed it was over eleven years old. He asked his wife, "Do you think the shoes will still be in the shop?" "Not likely," his wife said. "But it's worth a try."

Arnold drove to the shoe repair shop and, with a straight face, handed the ticket to the man behind the counter. The man looked at the ticket and said, "Just a minute. I'll have to go look for these." He disappeared to the back of the shop.

Two minutes later, the man called out, "Here they are!" "No kidding?" Arnold called back. "That's terrific! Who would have thought they'd still be here after all this time." The man came back to the counter and said, "They'll be ready on Thursday." [2]

How often do we put off and put off and put off what God has instructed us to do? We'll get around to it when we have more time or more money or when the kids are a little older. The fact of the matter is that we can always find excuses to procrastinate. Please don't wait any longer. Ask Jesus into your heart today.

"This is the day the LORD has made; let us rejoice and be glad in it" **(Psalm 118:24).**

Prayer: *Dear Lord, this challenge that you have laid on my heart—You know what I'm talking about—please help me not to put it off another day. Give me wisdom, courage, and discernment about how to start, and lead me to finish as You see fit. May I bring You joy this day as I accept the task you have put before me.*

Have you had your Joy Juice today? Excuses, excuses! Why do we waste time thinking up excuses? You know, an excuse is not a reason. It's just an explanation designed to avoid guilt or negative judgment.

Rudyard Kipling wrote, "We have forty million reasons for failure, but not a single excuse." [3] Excuses make us fall short of achieving our goals. In the spiritual context, making excuses demonstrates a lack of faith. When we're asked to serve and respond with "Oh, I can't do that!" and then give an excuse, we are not trusting God. We are limiting His ability to work through us.

Moses did exactly that when God told him that he was the man He had chosen to lead the Israelites out of Egypt. Moses didn't want the job, so he gave God his list of excuses. The first excuse is one that we all will recognize. Moses suggested that God had the wrong man for the job. He didn't feel qualified. Look what he said in **Exodus 3:11, 12: *"'Who am I, that I should go to Pharaoh and bring the Israelites out of Egypt?' And God said, 'I will be with you'."***

Has God ever given you a task that you felt you were unqualified to fulfill? Just as God answered Moses, He also says to us, "I will be with you." You see, what we lack, God will supply. Quit making excuses, and start spreading the joy of the Lord today.

Prayer: *Making excuses has become a habit, Lord. I'll admit that there are many things You have told me to do, and I have not been obedient. My good reasons are not anything but excuses. Please help me to trust You more and myself less. Show me that there is no excuse for sharing Your joy with others.*

Have you had your Joy Juice today? Are you listening? I asked, "Have you had your Joy Juice?"

Many times we find ourselves simply not listening. We tune things out. Maybe it's because we have so much on our minds or we're preoccupied with a problem. Sometimes we simply choose not to listen. Nevertheless, we have no good excuse when it comes to listening to God.

Here are a few important truths God is trying to tell us:

- I know the plans I have for you, plans to prosper you, not to harm you (Jer. 29:11).
- I will never leave you or forsake you (Heb. 13:5).
- You can do all things through Christ who gives you strength (Phil. 4:13).
- Ask and it will be given to you (Luke 11:9).
- I will supply all your needs (Phil. 4:19).

Do you hear what our Father is saying? Why don't we always listen to Him? Maybe for the same reason we choose not to read the directions on the box where it says "assembly required." The instructions are there, but we put them aside believing that we can do it on our own. After a while, we run into problems and maybe even get angry at the manu-facturer. Then as a last resort, we decide to read the instructions.

God should be our first resort, our first option. If we listen to His words of truth, trusting that He will do what he says, then we won't need to look for any excuses. We'll be following the directions toward a beautiful product called joy.

Prayers: *Okay, Lord, I know I've said it before, but I really mean it today. No more excuses! But I can't do this in my own strength. I'm depending on You. Let's go along this joyful journey together. I love You!*

Chapter Twelve

Keep On Keeping On Drinking that Joy Juice!

Have you had your Joy Juice today? Hope you are determined to persevere each day by remembering to drink your personal serving.

All of us have experienced discouragement (especially when we're tired and weak). Sometimes we feel like just sitting down and quitting. My grandmother used to have a poem hanging in her kitchen entitled "My Get-Up-And-Go Has Got Up And Went." I'm beginning to understand the sentiment behind those words more and more. We try to pack so much into our busy days that many times we are exhausted and overwhelmed.

Other times it's not really about how busy we are; it's the frame of mind we're in. Circumstances may arise that we had not anticipated. People may disappoint us. We may even disappoint ourselves by making poor choices and then having to suffer the consequences of those choices. When you feel like throwing in the towel, remember the verse in **Hebrews 10:36** that says, *"You need to persevere so that when you have done the will of God, you will receive what he has promised."*

"When you have done the will of God," the scripture says. We can't do the will of God if we don't know the will of God. And we can't know the will

of God unless we study His Word and listen to His voice. Bible study and prayer—that's where we start. But it takes a committed heart to persevere and make this a daily habit. Be diligent in finding and doing the will of God. This is a sure way to find renewed energy and to be filled with the joy of the Lord.

Prayer: *Dear Father, I do get so overwhelmed at times with all that's on my busy schedule. I am tempted sometimes just to quit. But I know that's not Your will. Help me to persevere to accomplish Your plan for my life. And fill me with Your energy and joy along the way.*

Have you had your Joy Juice today? You may need it to help you persevere through a busy, challenging day.

Is it possible to go through life with a joyful attitude, even during un-joyful times? **James 1:2, 3** tells us that we should "*Consider it pure joy, my brothers, whenever you face trials of many kinds, because you know that the testing of your faith develops perseverance.*"

We all go through heartache and trials. Many times God allows challenges in our lives for a bigger purpose than we can understand at the time. Think for moment about that trial you are facing right now. Whatever it is, it's important to God.

Consider the writer's words in the devotional *The Word for Today:*

He is weighing it in the light of your future. He has a plan in mind. **Romans 8:29** says, **"God knew [us] before he made the world, and he chose [us] to be like his Son"** Imagine that! One day we will be just like Jesus! "*In the coming ages*" (**Ephesians 2:7**) God is going to put us on display and say, "Look at My workmanship. Can you believe that

I made these glorified creatures from clay? When I first scooped them off the ground they wouldn't hold water. But I worked with them, molded them, put them through the fire and polished them up until they fulfilled my plan. They once were a disgrace and a disaster, but My grace was sufficient." [1]

That's just the kind of Joy Juice we all need to keep us encouraged to keep on keeping on.

Prayer: *Magnificent Creator God, it amazes me that with all You have to concern Yourself with, You still have time for me. You care about me so much that You continue to mold me and shape me. Indeed, You are the Potter, and I am the clay. Make of me what You have intended since before the beginning of time. I joyfully give my life back to You.*

Have you had your Joy Juice today? It's sure to help you not to feel so grouchy. We all have our grouchy days. But if you are finding yourself having more negative days than cheerful ones, then you're not persevering by drinking your joy juice.

Remember, people don't enjoy being around grouches. Unless, of course, your name is Slimy the Worm and you love Oscar the Grouch on Sesame Street. Oscar complains about everything. He has determined to be negative—never to be satisfied—to criticize everything people try to do for him. Now, we know that Oscar the Grouch is just a make-believe character, but I imagine many of you are smiling right now because you're thinking of a real live grouch. Am I right?

What can we do to help the grouches experience joy? The first thing is to simply set a good example. Smile a lot; say uplifting things; counter negative comments with positive ones. Model a joyful, Christian life, and when the timing is right, share Christ with them.

I know that's easier said than done some days. At times we need to step back, take a deep breath, and shoot up a flare prayer for God to give us wisdom and perseverance. Some people who we view as grouchy might be hurting or fearful. Pray that God would show you what you can do to express His love and joy in that person's life today. Tomorrow you might be the grouch who needs an extra serving of joy!

1 Thessalonians 5:16-18: *"Be joyful always; pray continually; give thanks in all circumstances, for this is God's will for you in Christ Jesus."*

Prayer: *Father, I am so thankful that You are never grouchy. You are always the same—ready to listen and help me in any way. Many times, I am the one who needs to examine my rotten attitude and remember to look to You for my example. Keep me joyful today, Lord, and help me to brighten someone's day with Your love.*

Have you had your Joy Juice today? Do you have any friends that are in need of a healthy serving today?

The story is told of Christian evangelist George Muller who began praying for five of his friends. After many months, one of them came to the Lord. Ten years later, two others were converted. It took twenty-five years before the fourth man was saved. Muller persevered in prayer until his death for the fifth friend, and throughout those fifty-two years, he never gave up hoping that his friend would accept Christ. His faith was rewarded, for soon after Muller's funeral the last one was saved. [2]

Perseverance is such an important quality, especially in our prayer life. Have you been praying for something for a while and are wondering why God hasn't answered your prayers? Remember what he tells us **Isaiah 55:8, 9:** "'*For my thoughts are not your thoughts, neither are your ways my ways,' declares the LORD. 'As the heavens are higher* *than the earth, so are my ways higher than your ways and my thoughts than your thoughts'."*

God knows what is best for us. We need to trust in his goodness and love. His timing is always perfect. No, our prayers may not be answered when we think they should be or even how we think they should be answered. But God is a lot wiser than we are, and He has a plan and a purpose for everything. So, don't get discouraged and be tempted to give up. Persevere! Keep on keeping on, and allow God to use you as an instrument of His promise and joy.

Prayer: *Father, lay on my heart today friends that need to know You as their personal Savior. Remind me to persevere in prayer for them. Also, let me be willing to be Your mouthpiece to lead them to Christ. Show me, lead me, and tenderize my heart to have such a burden for them that I will never stop praying for them. When they come to know You personally, Lord, I will be shouting with joy.*

Have you had your Joy Juice today? It's sure to help you finish with joy.

The old Timex slogan states, "It takes a licking and keeps on ticking." This sentiment should be a spiritual goal of every Christian. There aren't many who persevere with courage and determination these days. It's too easy to come up with excuses and bail out.

Let me tell you about a girl named Wilma who finished well:

A bout with polio left her left leg crooked and her foot twisted inward so she had to wear leg braces. After seven years of painful therapy, she learned to walk without her braces. At age twelve, Wilma tried out for a girls' basketball team but didn't make it. But she was determined. She practiced every day, and the next year she made the team. When a college track coach saw her during a game, he talked her into letting him train her as a runner. By age fourteen, she had outrun the fastest sprinters in the United States. In the 1960 Olympics in Rome, Wilma Rudolph won three gold medals, the most a woman had ever won. [3]

James 1:4 reminds us that *"Perseverance must finish its work so that you may be mature and complete, not lacking anything."* We are all going to face challenges. Perseverance is an essential quality for spiritual growth. Let's thank God for loving us so much that He gives us opportunities to grow closer to Him. He wants us to experience the joy that comes from persevering and allowing Him to finish His work in us. Let's strive to be a work of joy.

Prayer: *I desire, Father, to be "mature and complete." Help me never to give up pursuing a deeper relationship with You. That's the only way to have joy regardless of my circumstances. From this day forth, it is my goal to* ***"Rejoice in the Lord, always. I will say it again: Rejoice!"*** **(Phil. 4:4).**

ENDNOTES

Chapter One: Sip the Sweet Joy Juice of Jesus

1. Swindoll, Charles, *Swindoll's Ultimate Book of Illustrations & Quotes* (Nashville: Thomas Nelson, Inc, 1998), 322.

2. Swindoll, Charles, So, You *Want To Be Like Christ? Eight Essentials To Get You There* (Nashville: W Publishing Group, 2005), 9.

3. Shirer, Pricilla, *He Speaks to Me: Preparing to Hear From God* (Chicago: Moody Publishers, 2006), 111- 118.

4. Woolston, C. Herbert, "Jesus Loves the Little Children" (c. 1910).

5. *Life Application Bible NIV* (Wheaton: Tyndale House, 1988, 1989, 1990, 1991), 2143.

Chapter Two: Fresh and Fruity Joy Juice

1. *Life Application Bible NIV* (Wheaton: Tyndale House, 1988, 1989, 1990, 1991), 2125.

2. *Life Application Bible NIV* (Wheaton: Tyndale House, 1988, 1989, 1990, 1991), 2082-2083.

3. Jeremiah, David (http://www.davidjeremiah.org/site/magazine.aspx)

4. Hamilton, James, QuotationLibrary.com (Goodness).

5. Cotton, Roger D. *Paraclete*, Spring 1992, Vol. 26, No.2, pp. 27-32. Used with permission.

6. *God's Treasury of Virtues* (Tulsa: Honor Books, 1995) quote by Rev. James R. Miller, 302.

7. Horton, Stanley "Gentleness-Meekness" (www.enrichmentjournalag.org).

Chapter Three: Luscious Joy Juice:
The Libation of Love

1. Buscaglia, Leo. *Touching Stories about Children*
(www.healthy-communications.com/touching**storie**
saboutchildren.html)

2. Chapman, Gary. *The Five Love Languages*
(Chicago: Northfield Publishing, 1992, 1995), 119.

3. Warren, Rick. *The Purpose Driven Life* (Grand
Rapids: Zondervan, 2002), 231.

Chapter Four: Bitter Made Better

1. http://www.calvarychandler.net/Sermons/PDFs/8
_23_09.pdf, (August 22 & 23, 2009)

2. Renner, Rick, *Sparkling Gems from the Greek*
(Tulsa: Teach All Nations, 2003), 137-138.

3. *Life Application Bible NIV* (Wheaton: Tyndale
House, 1988, 1989, 1990, 1991), 2138.

4. Meyer, Joyce, *Reduce Me to Love, Unlocking the Secret to Lasting Joy* (New York: Faith Words, 2000), 43.

Chapter Five: Tart and Tangy Harvest-Flavored Joy Juice

1. http://news.aol.com/article/christy-harps-1725-pound-pumpkin-takes/707341

2. Excell, Edwin. *Songs for Young People,* (Chicago:1897), Oatman, Johnson, Jr., lyrics for "Count Your Many Blessings." (*www.cyberhymnal.org/htm/c/o/countyou.htm*)

Chapter Six: Warm Spiced Joy Juice Cider for the Christmas Holidays

1. Porter, Karen, *I'll Bring the Chocolate* (Colorado Springs: Multnomah Books, 2007), 51.

2. http://www.allaboutjesuschrist.org/origin-of-the-christmas-tree-faq.html "Origin of the Christmas Tree" (2002-2009).

3. http://www.just4kidsmagazine.com/poinsettia. html "The Legend of the Poinsettia" (December 2006).

4. http://www.homeschooled-kids.com/candycanele gend.html "The Legend of the Candy Cane" (1998-2007).

Chapter Seven: Joy Juice "Lite"

1. http://www.zoo.org/bflies_blms/facts.html.

Chapter Eight: Mama Mia! Now, that's Some Tasty Joy Juice!

1. Lewis, Jone Johnson, http://womenhistory.about. com/od/mothersday/a/anna_jarvis.htm "Mother's Day History".

2. "MOTHERHOOD: A Task Worth the Effort," *Women's Study Bible NKJV* (Nashville: Thomas Nelson Publishers, 1995), 1208.

3. http://quoteflections.blogspot.com/2009/05/mo thers-day-2009-top-ten-quotations.html.

4. http://www.quotationspage.com/quote/34271. html.

Chapter Nine: All Natural Joy Juice Smoothies

1. Weaver, Joanna. *Having a Mary Heart in a Martha World (Colorado Springs: Waterbrook Press, 2000, 2002),* 97.

2. McKinney, B.B. "Let Others See Jesus in You" (Nashville: Broadman Press, 1924, renewal 1952).

3. Hall, Steve, http://www.aboundingjoy.com/seeing Jesusinme.htm.

4. Cueto, Bernie. "Listening to Jesus in a Noisy World," April 10-13, 2006, http://www.pba.edu/chris tianlife/chapel/sermons-archives.cfm

Chapter Ten: Concentrated Joy Juice Squeezed from God's Word

1. *Life Application Bible NIV* (Wheaton: Tyndale House, 1988, 1989, 1990, 1991), Introduction to Psalms, 897.

2. Chambers, Oswald. *Bringing Sons unto Glory,* (Marshall, Morgan & Scott, 1943) http://www. crossroad.to/HisWord/notes/oswald/obedience.htm

3. *Life Application Bible NIV* (Wheaton: Tyndale House, 1988, 1989,1990,1991), Job 2:10 footnote, 844.

4. Keaggy, Cheri, *Because He First Loved Us,* "Restored" (www.cherikeaggy.com), Producer: Tom Hemby, PSALM 91 Records.

5. *http://www.thefreedictionary.com/good.*

Chapter Eleven: Drink up! No Excuses!!

1. Swindoll, Charles, *The Tale of the Tardy Oxcart And 1,501 Other Stories* (Nashville: Word, 1998), 189.

2. Crockett, Kent, *I Once Was Blind But Now I Squint,* (Chattanooga: MG Publishers, 2004), 1-2.

3. http://www.theatlantic.com/doc/191901/rightn ess-kipling.

Chapter Twelve: Keep On Keeping On Drinking That Joy Juice!

1. http://www.ucb.co.uk/index.cfm?itemid=88&test date=28%20Dec%202008.

2. http://www.christian-prayer-quotes.christian-at torney.net/.

3. *Today in the Word*, Moody Bible Institute, Jan, 1992, 10.

LaVergne, TN USA
11 January 2010
169599LV00001B/2/P

9 781615 796779